TREEHOUSES
and Other
COOL STUFF

TREEHOUSES
and Other
COOL STUFF
50 Projects You Can Build

David and Jeanie Stiles

Designs and Illustrations
by David Stiles

Gibbs Smith, Publisher
TO ENRICH AND INSPIRE HUMANKIND
Salt Lake City | *Charleston* | *Santa Fe* | *Santa Barbara*

First Edition
12 11 10 09 08   5 4 3 2 1

Published by
Gibbs Smith, Publisher
P.O. Box 667
Layton, Utah 84041

1-800.835.4993 orders
www.gibbs-smith.com

Designed and produced by David and Jeanie Stiles and Simon Jutras
Printed and bound in Canada

Library of Congress Cataloging-in-Publication Data

Stiles, David R.
   Treehouses and other cool stuff : 50 projects you can build / David and
Jeanie Stiles. -- 1st ed.
       p. cm.
   ISBN-13: 978-1-4236-0395-5
   ISBN-10: 1-4236-0395-8
   1. Tree houses. 2. Garden structures. 3. Furniture making. 4. Wooden toys.
I. Stiles, Jeanie II. Title. III. Title: Tree houses and other cool stuff.

 TH4885.S756 2008
 745.5--dc22
                                        2007043201

To grownup kids and grandkids everywhere, in the hope that
they build something that will make them smile.

Stiles Designs

Other Books by David and Jeanie Stiles

Treehouses & Playhouses You Can Build
Workshops You Can Build
Treehouses, Huts & Forts
Treehouses You Can Actually Build
Fun Projects for You and the Kids
Cabins: A Guide to Building Your own Retreat
Sheds: A Do-it-Yourself Guide, 3rd Edition
Playhouses You Can Build
Rustic Retreats
Garden Retreats

Please visit our Web site at
www.stilesdesigns.com
and send us photographs
of your projects.

To Our Readers

Since many of our readers invariably change our plans to fit their particular needs, we assume that they will seek qualified, licensed architects or engineers to make more detailed plans for submission to their local building and health departments, as required.

NOTE: Every effort has been made to design all the projects in this book to be safe and easy to build; however, it is impossible to predict every situation and the ability of each carpenter who builds our projects. Therefore, it is advised that the reader seek advice from a competent on-site expert.

Disclaimer: David and Jeanie Stiles make no express or implied warranties, including warranties of performance, merchantability and fitness for a particular purpose, regarding this information. Your use of this information is at your own risk. You assume full responsibility and risk of loss resulting from the use of this information. The authors and publisher will not be responsible for any direct, special, indirect, incidental, consequential or punitive damages or any other damage whatsoever.

Contents

Acknowledgments

Many thanks to Suzanne Taylor and Christopher Robbins for their confidence in our ability to produce a book and their enthusiasm for our building projects. And to Hollie Keith, the best editor we have encountered. And above all, to Simon Jutras, without whom we could not have completed this book as we envisioned it.

We also owe a debt of gratitude to our readers, who continue to inspire us with their ideas and suggestions, photos of their completed works and works in progress, and their words of encouragement and thanks—all of which have led to our writing yet another building book for them.

About This Book

If you are an adult, you may recognize many of these projects from your own childhood, like the lemonade stand, the raft and the model sailboat. We have picked projects we feel are timeless that appeal to kids of all ages and from all backgrounds. Who hasn't built a treehouse or at least dreamed of building one? The feeling of escape when camping out in the trees is something that can't be replicated by watching TV or working in front of a computer screen. In today's highly electronic world, filled with stress and daily deadlines, it's important to stretch your eyes to the horizon. Watching clouds or stars overhead and being a part of nature creates lasting memories.

Treehouses and Other Cool Stuff is filled with fifty hands-on projects that give kids and their parents a chance to work together. We have divided the projects into levels of difficulty, with symbols of hammers at the beginning of each project. One-hammer projects are easy and quick to build while four-hammer projects are more challenging and time-consuming. Two- and three-hammer projects fall in between. Each project is accompanied by hand-drawn, easy-to-follow illustrations.

The book begins with some carpentry basics and building tips, like making your own saw guide and a kid-size sawhorse, that will make the rest of your building projects go more smoothly. Some projects take less than an hour to build (for instance, the Cootie Catcher and Noisemaker) while others may take a summer, such as the Monster House.

The section "Huts, Treehouses & Playhouses" includes two treehouses—one is a Tree Fort and the other a simpler treeless A-frame Treehouse. These projects include detailed plans, illustrations and materials lists from nuts to bolts. Other projects in this section, like the Monster House and the Ad Hoc Tree Fort, are included as inspirational designs only. We encourage you to use your own creativity, imagination, resources and skills to build something unique, using the building techniques that we have included.

In response to the many e-mails that we have received from past readers of our other books, we have also included sections on "Treehouse Accessories" and "Stuff to Do in Your Treehouse." When you finish building your treehouse, you might start your own band, using the instructions for making simple musical instruments.

The book also contains projects that can be done in one weekend, like the Exploding Cannon and the Wheel of Fortune. The chapter "Things That Move" includes projects that will appeal to all active kids, especially the Downhill Racer and the Recycled Raft.

Whenever possible, we have tried to design projects to use the least amount of expensive materials and encourage you to use or substitute materials you already have. Many of the projects (like the Ski Sled, Downhill Racer and Box Sled) can be made from recycled materials found around the house. We also expect our readers to adapt our plans and designs to suit their situation and, above all, to be inventive. We hope you enjoy building these projects as much as we did.

Carpentry Basics

Kids, Build This First Sawhorse

This is not just a sawhorse. It can also be used as a kid's workbench or a handy footstool for adults.

To determine the height, measure the distance from the floor to your child's waist when he or she is standing up. The width of the legs should be greater than the height of the sawhorse to prevent it from tipping.

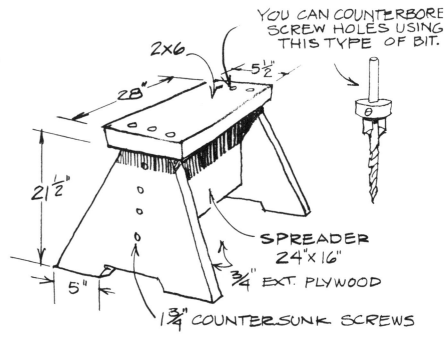

YOU CAN COUNTERBORE SCREW HOLES USING THIS TYPE OF BIT.

2x6

28"

5½"

21½"

5"

SPREADER 24"x16"

¾" EXT. PLYWOOD

1¾" COUNTERSUNK SCREWS

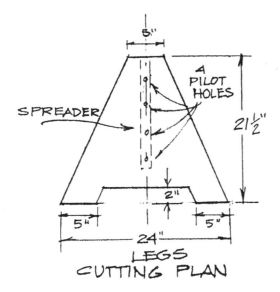

SPREADER

4 PILOT HOLES

5"

21½"

2"

5"   24"   5"

LEGS CUTTING PLAN

Cut the top from a scrap piece of 2x6. Cut the legs and the spreader from 3/4-inch exterior plywood. Drill pilot holes before gluing and screwing the pieces together. Counterbore the screws in the top so they will not come in contact with the saw when you are cutting lumber. When the top gets too worn, unscrew it and replace it with another 2x6 top.

TOOLBOX

In preparation for building any project, it's a good idea to have a toolbox handy, filled with all the necessary tools. The one shown here is a slightly smaller version of the one used by most professional carpenters. It is made out of one 1x4 and one 1x8 board. The handle can be made from an old broomstick or a 1-inch-diameter dowel.

When outfitting the toolbox, buy a saw that is 15 inches long (see **Resources**) and make sure that it has small teeth (at least 12 teeth per inch) to make sawing easier for kids.

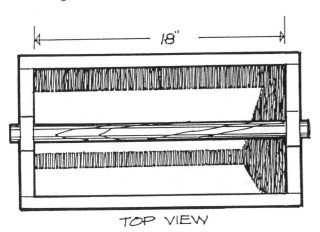

18"

TOP VIEW

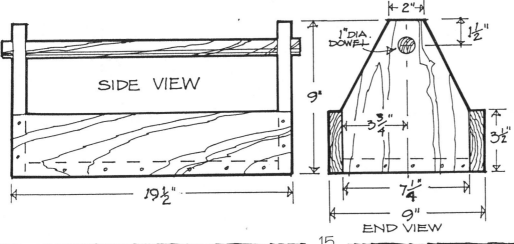

SIDE VIEW

19½"

2"

1" DIA. DOWEL

1½"

9"

3¾"

3½"

7¼"

9"

END VIEW

How to Make a Saw Guide

It is almost impossible to accurately cut plywood panels or long boards without using a straight edge. The saw guide shown below can be made in just a few minutes and lasts a lifetime.

- Choose a very straight 1/2 x 3-inch board and an 8-foot-long piece of plywood, 10 to 12 inches wide.
- Screw the 1/2 x 3-inch board to the plywood to act as a fence for the saw to slide against.
- To custom fit this guide to match your particular saw, place the saw on the plywood and while pressing the base of the saw against the 1/2 X 3-inch fence, cut off the excess plywood.

To use the saw guide, nail or screw it to the piece you want to cut. Make sure to allow for the thickness of the saw blade before you cut the plywood.

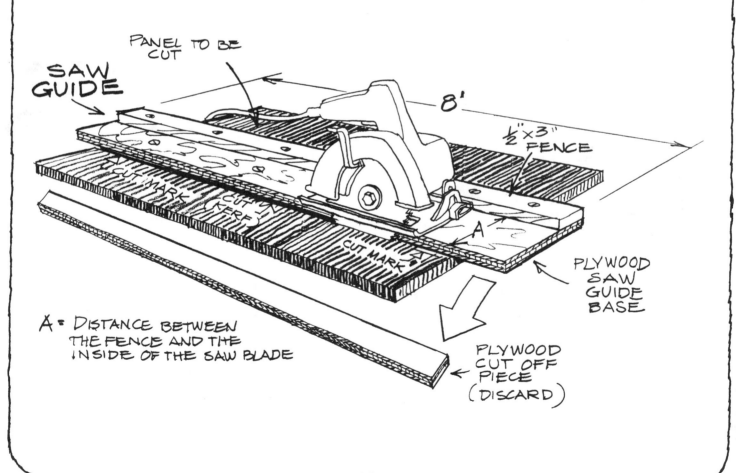

SAW GUIDE

PANEL TO BE CUT

8'

1/2"x3" FENCE

A

PLYWOOD SAW GUIDE BASE

A = DISTANCE BETWEEN THE FENCE AND THE INSIDE OF THE SAW BLADE

PLYWOOD CUT OFF PIECE (DISCARD)

How to Crosscut a Board

Making an accurate crosscut through a board is not as easy as it looks. Here are some useful tips to help you:

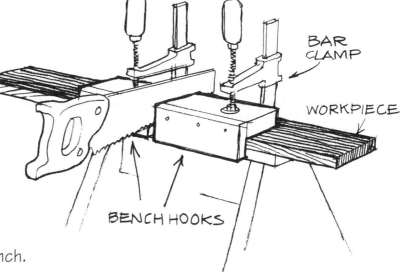

- Choose a saw that is neither too long nor too short. Fifteen inches is just right for an amateur carpenter. The saw should have teeth that cut on both the backstroke and the forward stroke, with about 12 teeth to the inch.

- Use a square to mark the workpiece with a pencil. Make 2 lines—one for the actual cut line and one on the waste side, the same width as the saw blade.

- To keep the workpiece steady while you are working, clamp the board to the sawhorse. Make 2 bench hooks out of 2x4s and 1x4s. Clamp the bench hooks over the cut line with just enough room for the saw blade to fit through without binding.

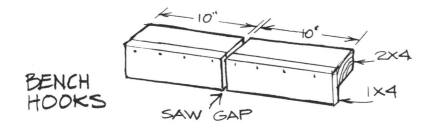

Carpentry Tips

Pilot Holes

What is a pilot hole? A pilot hole is the hole that you drill before you attach a screw or a nail that makes it easier to drill or hammer through the wood. It helps the screw go in easier and the nail go in straighter. A pilot hole should be slightly smaller than the diameter of the screw or nail. When drilling into hardwood, drill an additional smaller pilot hole into the hardwood to help get the screw started.

Use a large spade bit or counterbore bit to recess bolts that might extend from the wood and possibly injure someone. In this case, drill this hole first before drilling a pilot hole.

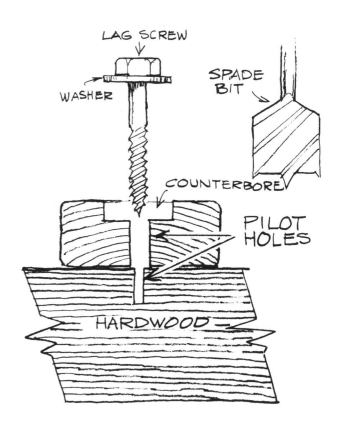

LAG SCREW

WASHER

SPADE BIT

COUNTERBORE

PILOT HOLES

HARDWOOD

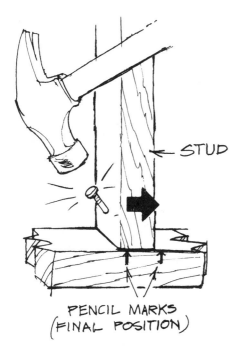

STUD

PENCIL MARKS (FINAL POSITION)

Toenailing

When toenailing, begin by placing the stud 1/4 inch away from the desired location. Start the nail at an angle and begin hammering it in. Your last few strokes will knock the stud over to its final location.

Note: Use 16-pound 3 1/2-inch nails. (Four nails recommended.)

Huts,
Treehouses &
Playhouses

Tree Fort

If you have only one tree, this design is a good choice. Two posts and knee braces provide the additional support necessary. Wise grandparents built this sturdy treehouse for their grandkids to gather in each summer, where they can camp out surrounded by branches, birds and a view of the lake. The windows have screens and there's room for several sleeping bags inside.

Materials List

Note: All dimensions are approximate and should be adjusted for each builder's specific situation.

Qty.	Description	Length	Location
Platform			
(2)	2x6 #2 D. fir*	10'	V-knee brace
(4)	2x8 #2 D. fir	10'	floor frame
(7)	2x6	10'	floor joists
(2)	4x4 #2 cedar or ACQ	15'	posts
(1)	4x4	12'	knee brace and rail posts
(2)	AC plywood	4'x4'	interior floor
(9)	5/4 x 6	#2 cedar	decking

*D. Fir = Douglas fir

Qty.	Description	Length	Location
Stairs			
(2)	2x6 clear cedar	10'	stringers
(1)	2x6 clear cedar	16'	treads

Qty.	Description	Length	Location
House			
(1)	4x4 #2 cedar	10'	rear corner posts
(4)	2x4 #2 cedar	8'	sill plates
(7)	2x4 #2 cedar	10'	rear and side wall studs
(3)	2x4 #2 cedar	10'	front wall studs
(6)	2x4 #2 cedar	8'	top plates
(2)	2x6 #2 cedar	8'	front header
(4)	2x4 #2 cedar	8'	cats
(4)	3/8" Lauan ply.	4'x8'	wall sheathing
(6)	5/4 x 4 # 2 cedar	10'	corners and door trim
(2)	18" bundles Perfection shingles #1 cedar shingles		walls

Gabled Roof

(8)	2x6 #2 cedar	12'	rafters and fascia
(1)	2x6 #2 cedar	12'	ridgepole
(20)	1x4 #2 pine	8'	nailers
(1)	2x4 #2 cedar	12'	gable frame
(1)	1x4 #2 cedar	16'	trim to cover insect screen
(1)	5/4 x 6 cedar	14'	header trim
(7)	24" bundles hand-split cedar shakes		roofing
(1)	roll 30-lb. tar paper		roof
(1)	36" wide roll		insect screen for gables and windows

Windows

(1)	2x3 spruce	16'	front windows
(4)	2x3 spruce	10'	side windows
(8)	pair screen hooks		
(8)	screw eyes and hooks		

Door

(3)	1x6 T&G clear cedar	10'	door and battens
(2)	decorative wrought-iron strap hinges		
(1)	decorative wrought-iron thumb-latch handle		

Fasteners and Hardware

Nails, lag screws, joist hangers, hinges
Optional: 1 gallon Cabot grey stain

AC ply = A/C grade exterior plywood
ACQ = pressure treated
O.C. = on center
P.T. = pressure treated
TYP = typical

Find a tree that is at least 10 inches in diameter and attach a 2x6 x 9 1/2-foot-long beam to it using a 5/8 x 5-inch lag screw. Support the beam by attaching two 2x6 x 5-foot braces to form a "V."

Drop a plumb bob from both beam-ends to the ground and measure two 7-foot-long parallel lines, marking where the 2 posts will go. Check the diagonal measurements to make sure they are equal. Dig two 12-inch-wide holes, 36 inches deep, and place two 4x4 cedar or pressure-treated posts loosely in the holes. Do not backfill the holes until the floor is framed.

Build the floor frame out of 2x6s and attach it to the posts using 1/2 x 6-inch galvanized bolts.

Before backfilling the holes, make sure that the posts are plumb. For rigidity, add two 4x4 x 5-foot-long knee braces, as shown.

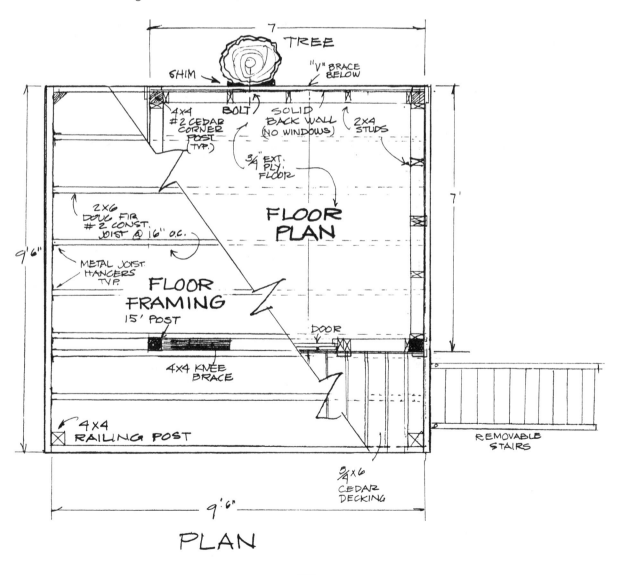

PLAN

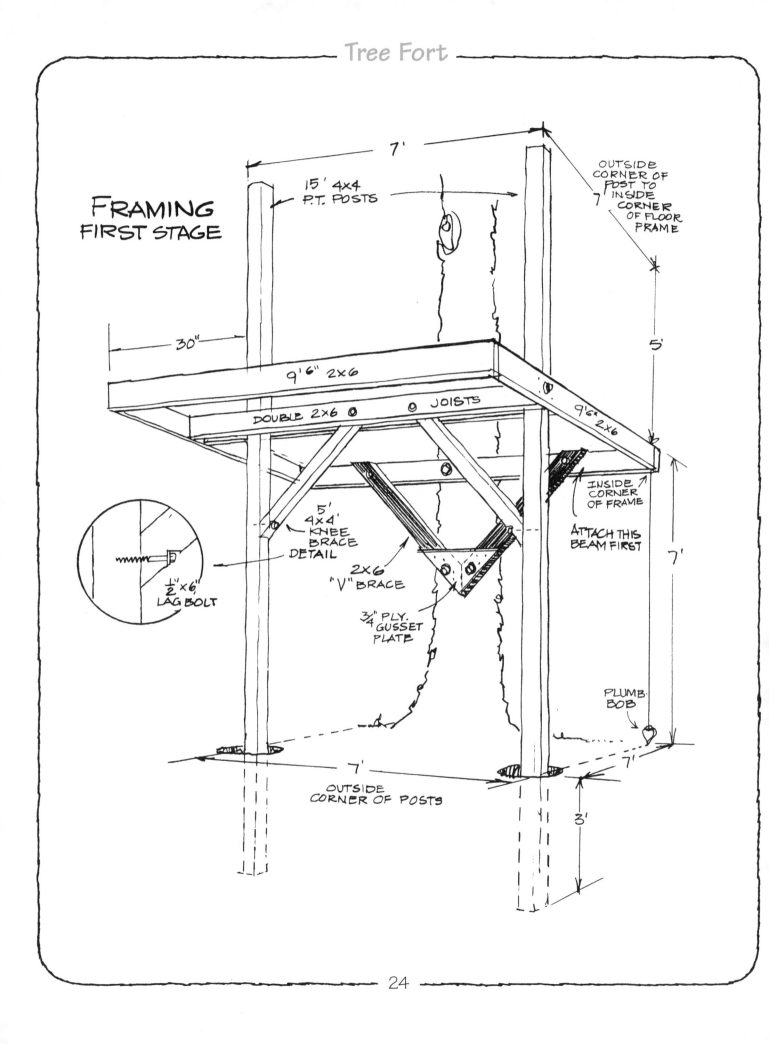

FRAMING
FIRST STAGE

7'

15' 4x4
P.T. POSTS

OUTSIDE
CORNER OF
POST TO
INSIDE
CORNER
OF FLOOR
FRAME

7'

30"

9'6" 2x6

5'

DOUBLE 2x6   JOISTS

9'6" 2x6

INSIDE
CORNER
OF FRAME

ATTACH THIS
BEAM FIRST

5'
4x4'
KNEE
BRACE
DETAIL

2x6
"V" BRACE

3/4" PLY.
GUSSET
PLATE

7'

1/2" x6"
LAG BOLT

PLUMB
BOB

7'

7'

OUTSIDE
CORNER OF POSTS

3'

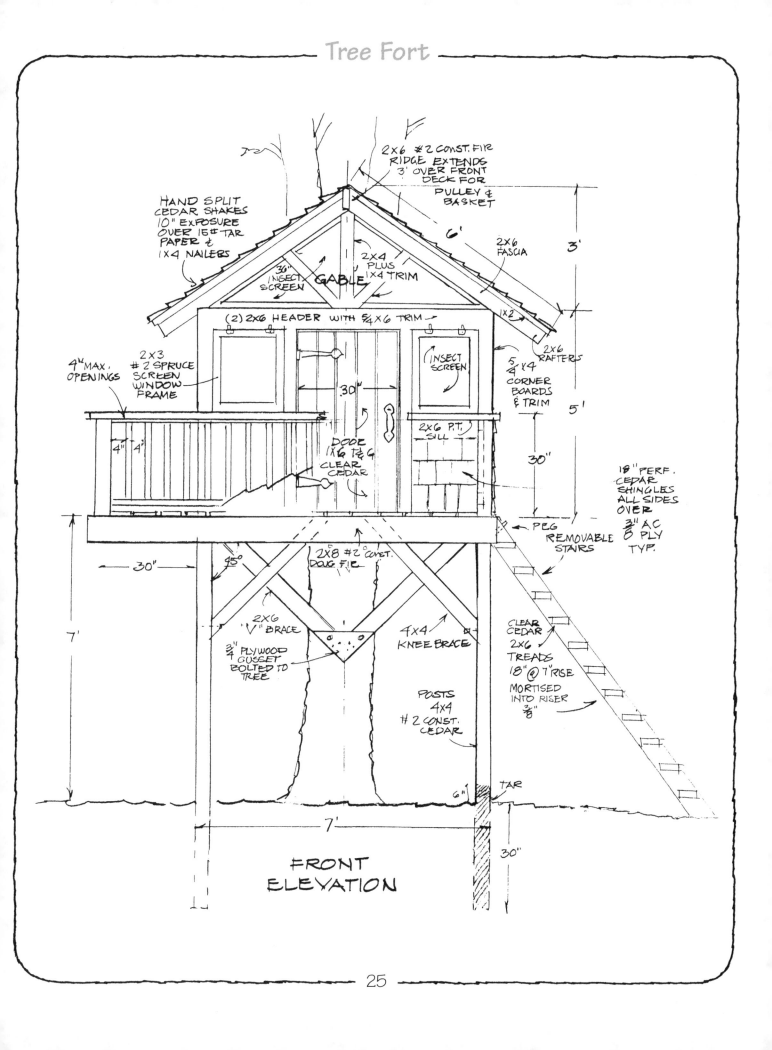

HAND SPLIT
CEDAR SHAKES
10" EXPOSURE
OVER 15# TAR
PAPER &
1X4 NAILERS

2X6 #2 CONST. FIR
RIDGE EXTENDS
3' OVER FRONT
DECK FOR
PULLEY &
BASKET

2X6
FASCIA

3'

6'

36"
INSECT
SCREEN

GABLE

2X4
PLUS
1X4 TRIM

1X2

(2) 2X6 HEADER WITH 5/4X6 TRIM

2X6
RAFTERS

5'

4" MAX.
OPENINGS

2X3
#2 SPRUCE
SCREEN
WINDOW
FRAME

30"

INSECT
SCREEN

5/4 X4
CORNER
BOARDS
& TRIM

30"

4" 4"

DOOR
1X6 T&G
CLEAR
CEDAR

2X6 P.T.
SILL

18" PERF.
CEDAR
SHINGLES
ALL SIDES
OVER
3" AC
8 PLY
TYP.

PEG

REMOVABLE
STAIRS

30"

45°

2X8 #2 CONST.
DOUG FIR

7'

2X6
"V" BRACE

3/4" PLYWOOD
GUSSET
BOLTED TO
TREE

4X4
KNEE BRACE

CLEAR
CEDAR
2X6
TREADS
18" @ 7"RISE
MORTISED
INTO RISER
3/8"

POSTS
4X4
#2 CONST.
CEDAR

6"

TAR

30"

FRONT
ELEVATION

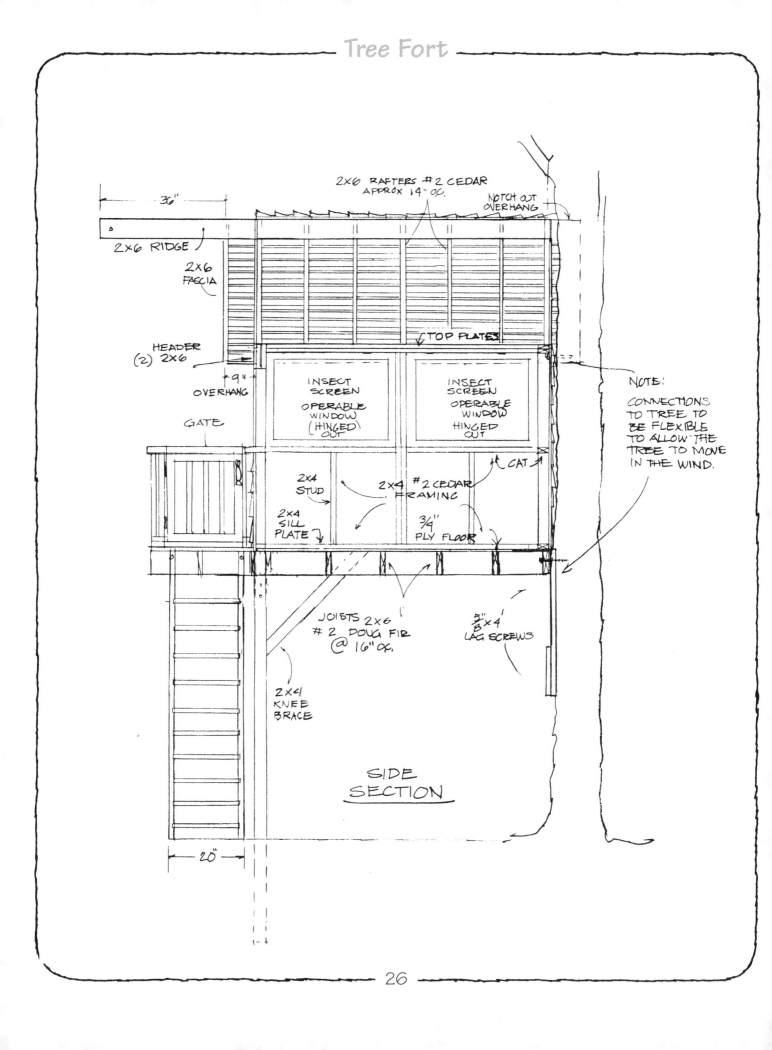

2X6 RAFTERS #2 CEDAR
APPROX 14" OC.

NOTCH OUT
OVERHANG

36"

2X6 RIDGE

2X6
FAECIA

HEADER
(2) 2X6

9"
OVERHANG

TOP PLATES

GATE

INSECT
SCREEN
OPERABLE
WINDOW
(HINGED
OUT)

INSECT
SCREEN
OPERABLE
WINDOW
HINGED
OUT

NOTE:

CONNECTIONS
TO TREE TO
BE FLEXIBLE
TO ALLOW THE
TREE TO MOVE
IN THE WIND.

CAT

2X4
STUD

2X4 #2 CEDAR
FRAMING

2X4
SILL
PLATE

3/4"
PLY FLOOR

JOISTS 2X6
#2 DOUG FIR
@ 16" OC.

3/8"X4'
LAG SCREWS

2X4
KNEE
BRACE

SIDE
SECTION

20"

A-Frame Tree House

This A-frame treehouse can be built using 1 tree and 2 posts or using 4 posts for supports. It is constructed using 4x8-foot plywood sheets. Shingling over the plywood is optional.

Materials list for treehouse using 4 posts:

Qty.	Description	Length	Location
(4)	4x4 ACQ posts	10'	support posts
(7)	2x6 #2 fir	8'	floor frame
(1)	3/4-inch ext. ply.	4'x8' sheet	floor
(6)	5/4 x 6 cedar	8'	deck
(2)	2x4 cedar	10'	knee braces
(1)	4x4 cedar	8'	railing posts
(4)	5/8" ext. ply.	4'x8' sheets	roof, front and back sides
(14)	2x3 spruce	8'	framing
(1)	2x4 fir	12'	ridge board
(2)	2x6 cedar	8'	railing
(8)	2x2 cedar	8'	balustrades
(4)	11/16" x 1 3/8" solid crown molding	9'	roof edging
(3)	2x6 cedar	8'	ladder
(2)	1x4 cedar	8'	ladder step supports
(4)	80-lb. bags sacrete		post footings
(4)	3" galvanized butt hinges		windows

AC ply. = A/C grade exterior plywood
Ext. ply. = exterior plywood
ACQ = pressure treated
T1-11 ply = textured 1-11 plywood
o.c. = on center
i.d. = inside dimension
Optional: Asphalt shingles for treehouse roof.

Note: If you shingle your treehouse, use staples instead of nails to attach shingles.

Clear your building site from brush and rocks and mark out an area with string that is 89 1/2 inches wide and 66 1/2 inches deep. This represents the exact center of where the 4 posts will go. Check the diagonal measurements from corner to corner to make sure they measure the same. Dig 4 holes where the strings intersect, 12 inches wide and 36 inches deep. Place the 10-foot-long 4x4s in the holes loosely. Don't backfill until the frame is in place. Temporarily brace the posts to keep them plumb.

FLOOR PLAN PLATFORM

8'

89½" o.c.

24"

24" o.c.   24" o.c.   24"

36" 2x4 KNEE BRACES

¾" EXT. PLY FLOOR

66¾" o.c.

7'

2x6 CONST. FIR JOISTS 24 o.c.

20"

5/4×6 #2 CEDAR DECKING

DECK

4x4 P.T. 10' SUPPORT POST

4x4 DECK RAILING POST

2x2 ANGLE FLASHING

2x4 RIDGE BEAM & BRACE

5/8" T1-11 PLY. ROOF OR 5/8" EXT. PLY.

36"

24"

WINDOW HINGE

PROP

PORTHOLE WINDOW ½" PLY.

CEDAR 2x6 CEDAR RAILING

1x4 STOP

⅛" Acrylic PANE

2x2 CEDAR

4x4 RAILING POST

1x6 T&G CEDAR

24"

24"

24"

6"

24"

5/8" T1-11 PLY. OR 5/8" EXT. PLY.

2x6 LADDER

2x4 x 3' KNEE BRACE

2" OVERHANG

FRONT VIEW

Build the 2x6 frame 7 feet deep and 8 feet wide (see floor plan of platform), and lift the platform frame over the posts. Level the platform frame and attach it to the posts with two 3/8 x 4-inch lag screws at each joint. Add the 36-inch 2x4 braces to the posts and frame. When everything fits plumb and level, fill in the holes with soil. **Important:** Tamp down the soil as you add each shovelful, using a 2x4. Fill the last 8 to 10 inches of the hole with concrete and allow it to cure for 24 hours.

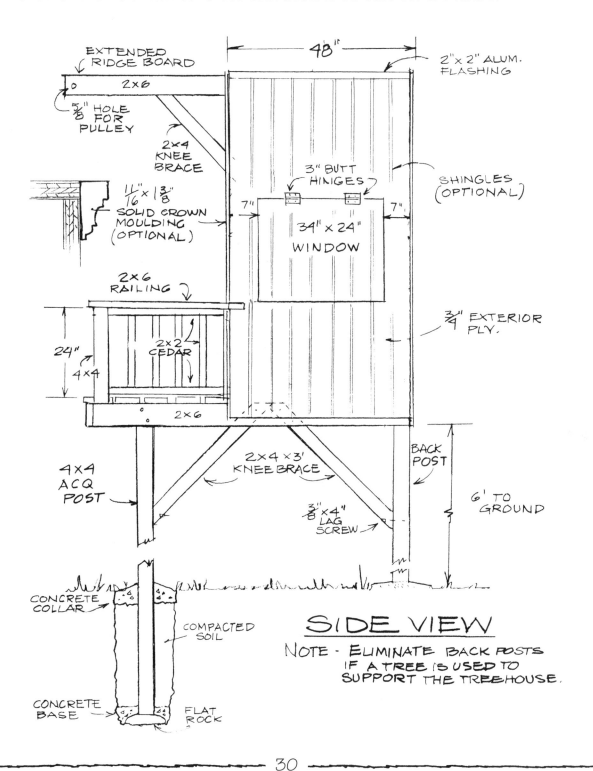

EXTENDED RIDGE BOARD

2x6

48"

2" x 2" ALUM. FLASHING

5/8" HOLE FOR PULLEY

2x4 KNEE BRACE

3" BUTT HINGES

SHINGLES (OPTIONAL)

$\frac{11}{16}$" x $1\frac{3}{8}$" SOLID CROWN MOULDING (OPTIONAL)

7"

7"

34" x 24" WINDOW

2x6 RAILING

3/4" EXTERIOR PLY.

24"

4x4

2x2 CEDAR

2x6

BACK POST

4x4 ACQ POST

2x4 x 3' KNEE BRACE

3/8" x 4" LAG SCREW

6' TO GROUND

CONCRETE COLLAR

COMPACTED SOIL

CONCRETE BASE

FLAT ROCK

SIDE VIEW

NOTE - ELIMINATE BACK POSTS IF A TREE IS USED TO SUPPORT THE TREEHOUSE.

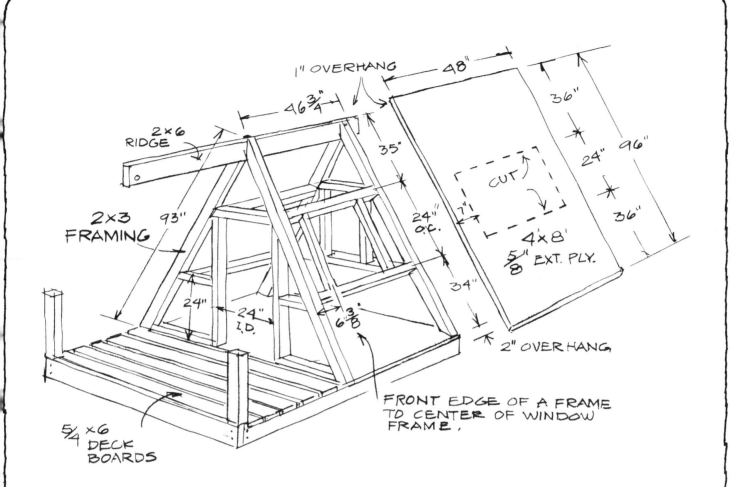

Framing

Cover the floor joists with 3/4-inch exterior plywood and the front deck with 5/4 x 6 deckboards.

Build the frame using 2x3s, as shown in the illustration.

Cut the roof panels out of 5/8-inch exterior plywood. Allow the bottom roof panels to overhang the floor panel by 2 inches.

Cut and nail the front and rear panels to the frame, leaving a 24-inch-wide space for the door.

Build the railing out of 2x6s and 2x2s, leaving a 20-inch space for access via ladder or stairs.

Details

Door (optional)

Make a Dutch door out of 4 pieces of 1x8 tongue-and-groove cedar backed with 1x6 battens. Make a "porthole" window by cutting a 10-inch-diameter hole in the top door and a 13 1/2-inch-diameter circle out of 1/2-inch exterior plywood. Cut and screw a 10-inch-diameter disk, made from 1/8-inch clear Plexiglas, to the back of the 1/2-inch plywood port-hole. Screw the porthole to the door.

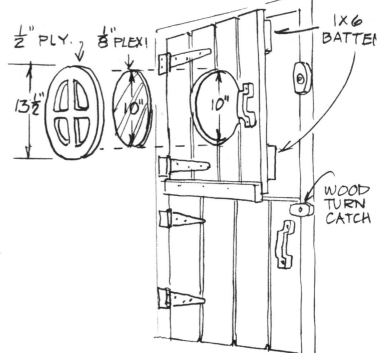

STEP SUPPORT
1x4 CLEAT
1/2" DIAMETER PEG
2x6

Stairs

Build the stairs out of 2x6s. Support each step with 1x4 cleats, as shown. Attach the stairs to the treehouse with 1/2-inch-diameter pegs so that they can be removed, if necessary.

Knee Braces

Cut the 36-inch-long knee braces from 2x4s. Screw the top of the brace to the inside of the floor frame and screw the bottom to the posts, using 3/8 x 6-inch galvanized lag screws.

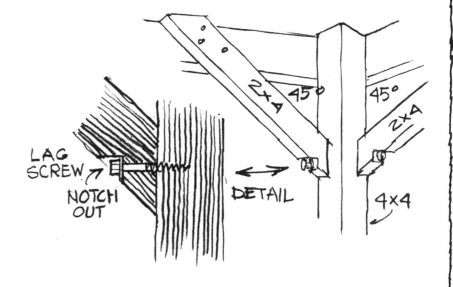

LAG SCREW
NOTCH OUT
2x4 45°
45° 2x4
DETAIL
4x4

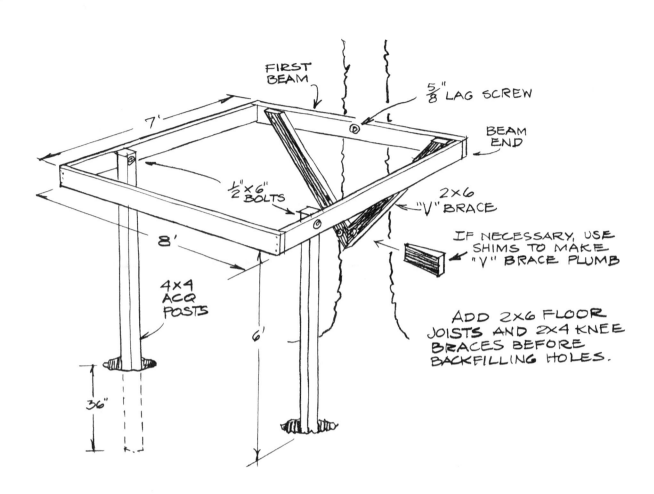

FIRST BEAM

7'

$\frac{1}{2}$"X6" BOLTS

8'

4X4 ACQ POSTS

36"

6'

$\frac{5}{8}$" LAG SCREW

BEAM END

2X6 "V" BRACE

IF NECESSARY, USE SHIMS TO MAKE "V" BRACE PLUMB

ADD 2X6 FLOOR JOISTS AND 2X4 KNEE BRACES BEFORE BACKFILLING HOLES.

A-Frame Treehouse Using 1 Tree and 2 Posts for Support

You can adapt a treehouse supported by 4 posts by eliminating the 2 back posts and adding the V-brace, as shown above.

Find a tree that is at least 10 inches in diameter and attach a 2x6 x 8-foot beam to it using a 5/8 x 5-inch lag screw. Support the beam ends by attaching two 2x6 x 4-foot braces to form a "V."

Dig two 36-inch-deep, 12-inch-wide holes in front of the beam-ends and place two 4x4 cedar or pressure-treated posts loosely in the holes. Do not backfill the holes until the floor is framed.

Build the floor frame out of 2x6s and attach it to the posts using 1/2 x 6-inch galvanized bolts.

Before backfilling the holes, make sure that the posts are plumb. For rigidity, add two 2x4 x 3-foot-long knee braces, as shown.

Nature Hut

This hut can be made using only material found in the woods (with the exception of the string). This type of shelter may have been one of the first dwellings constructed by man. For tools, all you need is a small pruning saw to cut the branches.

In the woods, find 2 saplings that are growing together, about 6 feet apart. Bend them over and tie them together with thin rope.

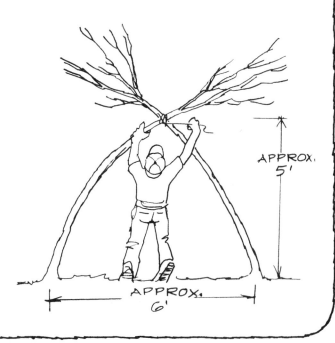

1" DIAMETER

APPROX. 5'

APPROX. 6'

RIDGEPOLE

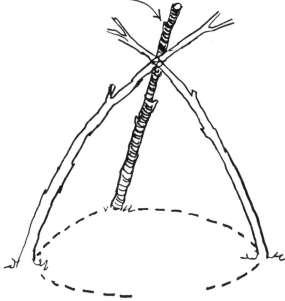

Add a ridgepole to the back and tie it to the 2 saplings.

Add more saplings or long, straight branches to the structure. Once that is done, tie horizontal sticks to the saplings to create a frame.

Cover the frame with pine boughs, twigs and leaves to create a camouflaged secret hut.

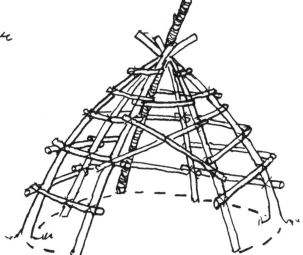

SLANTED UPRIGHTS, APPROXIMATELY 1" IN DIAMETER.

Swinging Treehouse

This treehouse is suspended between 2 trees using 3/4-inch-diameter nylon rope. Samson Rope Technologies makes a 3-strand nylon rope that they describe as having a safe working load of 2,700 pounds. It is available through Defender Marine & Boat Supplies (see **Resources**).

Note: Use only Dacron or nylon rope. Check connections yearly, and make sure the rope has not frayed.

Making the Platform

Trace a 2x4 shape in the corner of the 4x4 plywood and cut it out for later use.

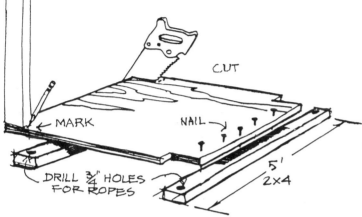

MARK

CUT

NAIL

5'
2x4

DRILL ¾" HOLES
FOR ROPES

To strengthen and add support to the treehouse, screw two 5-foot-long 2x4s to the underside of the plywood floor.

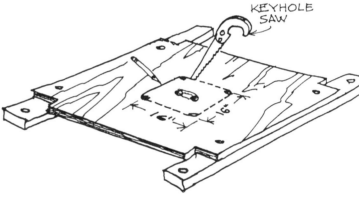

KEYHOLE SAW

16"

16"

Cut out the 16 x 16-inch access door and a 4 x 1-inch hand hole.

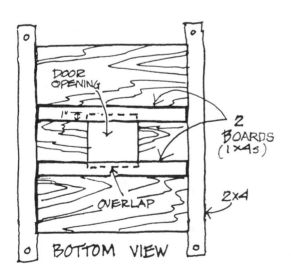

DOOR OPENING

1"

2
BOARDS
(1x4s)

OVERLAP

2x4

BOTTOM VIEW

To keep the door from falling through, screw two 1x4 boards across the bottom so they overlap the door opening by 1 inch.

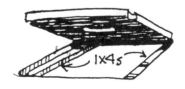

1x4s

LARGE NAIL

Raising the Floor Platform

Select 2 trees about 10 feet apart. Tie the end of a rope through one of the corner holes in the floor platform and wrap the rope around one of the trees. Place it 4 to 5 feet higher than where you want the treehouse floor to be. To keep the rope from slipping down, hammer a large nail into the back of the tree and let the rope rest on it.

5 ft.

Wrap the rope around the tree a couple of times and tie the loose end to the other hole on the same side of the floor platform.

Repeat the same step on the other side. Take up the slack, alternating between one side and the other until the floor platform is centered between the 2 trees. When the floor platform is level, hammer several thin nails through the rope and into the back of the tree to lock it in place.

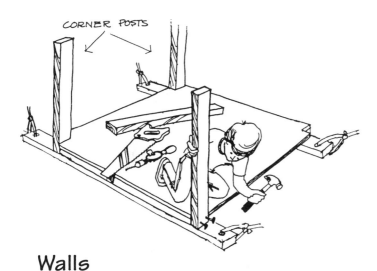

CORNER POSTS

Walls

Cut 4 pieces of 2x4s into 3-foot lengths and screw them into the corners.

Tip: Drill pilot holes for the screws first.

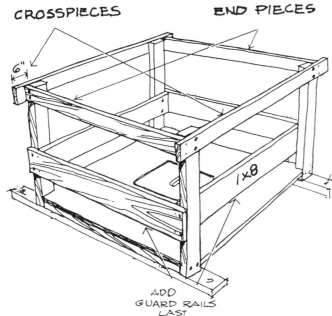

CROSSPIECES   END PIECES

6"

1x8

ADD
GUARD RAILS
LAST

Wall Frame

- Cut 2 top 1x4 crosspieces, overlapping the ends by 6 inches.

- Add the four 1x8 guard boards next.

Roof

- Cut 3 pieces of 5/4 x 4s into 5-foot lengths.

- Notch and cut off 2 of them at an angle, as shown.

- Fit the third piece (the roof ridge) into the notches.

- Nail the roof supports to the end pieces.

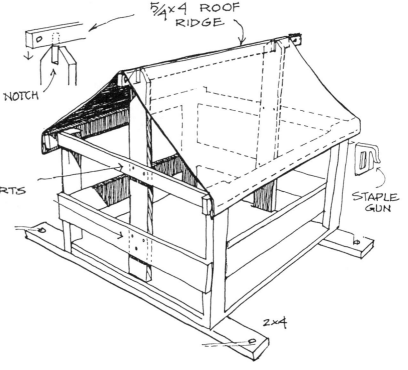

5/4x4 ROOF RIDGE

NOTCH

NAIL THE
ROOF SUPPORTS
TO THE END
PIECES.

STAPLE GUN

2x4

Roofing

- Cut a piece of canvas to measure 4 x 7 feet and staple it to the frame.

Monster House

Imagine walking through the woods and coming upon this creature, groaning and waving his arms at you! We've drawn this monster house to inspire you to imagine and build your own unique creature. Using these building techniques, you can build almost anything. This type of construction is a 4-hammer challenge and meant only for the adventurous, skilled carpenter with plenty of time.

You can access this monster through his back by means of a rope ladder that can be pulled up in case of an attack by earthlings. It has 2 levels, which share a front window for lighting the inside. The monster's arms are made of flexible heating duct and can be waved by pulling on a hidden rope. Make the hand out of an old baseball mitt.

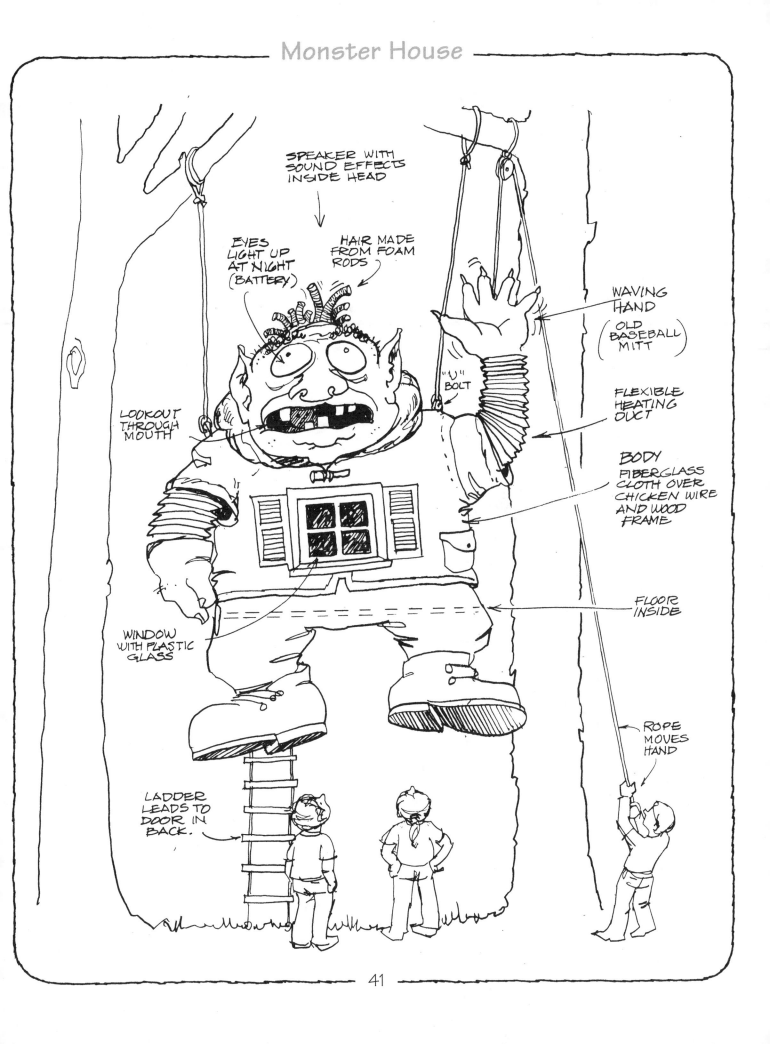

PLYWOOD FRAME

Using this method, you can build the frame gradually by cutting short pieces of 1/2-inch plywood and gluing and screwing them together to form 1-inch-thick ribs. This construction method allows you to unscrew and re-cut pieces that don't fit quite right the first time and also prevents you from wasting plywood.

1"

DOUBLE ½" PLYWOOD

3"

APPROXIMATELY 5'-WIDE × 4' DEEP OVAL

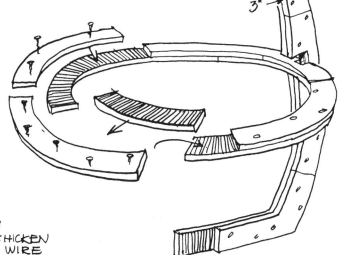

6" DIA. PLEXIGLAS DOME

ELECTRIC LAMP (BATTERY)

SECTION

EYE

1/8" COPPER WIRE

1" CHICKEN WIRE OVER WIRE

HANGING U-BOLT

ADD ARMS USING FLEXIBLE HEATING DUCT.

WINDOW

After you have finished building the basic plywood frame, staple 1/8-inch-diameter copper wire to the plywood and cover with 1-inch chicken wire. Cover this frame with burlap saturated with plaster and sculpt details like ears, nose, lips, etc., with more plaster. Let the plaster dry for 24 hours and cover the entire structure with lightweight fiberglass cloth. Cover with 3 coats of Polyester resin.

Add translucent eyes, a plastic window (see **Resources**) and a rear access door. Paint to suit. Hang the monster between 2 trees, using two U-bolts.

Tip: For more inspirational creatures, go to Google on your computer and type in "Theo Jensen's Kinetic Sculpture."

Dragon House

You can build the frame of this dragon playhouse out of lattice and chicken wire. Cover the chicken wire with burlap cloth dipped in wet plaster. Sculpt the final details using clay or Structolite and add a protective covering of lightweight fiberglass dipped in polyester resin. Using this method, you can build almost anything—a turtle, a hippo, a snail or a creature purely from your imagination.

FRAME

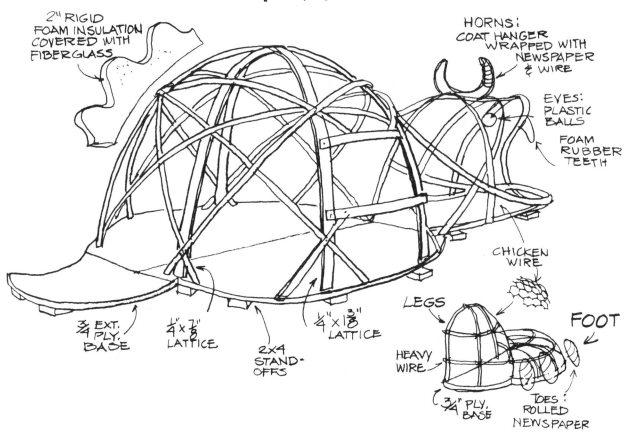

2" RIGID FOAM INSULATION COVERED WITH FIBERGLASS

HORNS: COAT HANGER WRAPPED WITH NEWSPAPER & WIRE

EYES: PLASTIC BALLS

FOAM RUBBER TEETH

CHICKEN WIRE

LEGS

FOOT

HEAVY WIRE

3/4" PLY. BASE

TOES: ROLLED NEWSPAPER

3/4 EXT. PLY. BASE

1/4" x 7/8" LATTICE

2x4 STAND-OFFS

1/4" x 1 3/8" LATTICE

COVERING

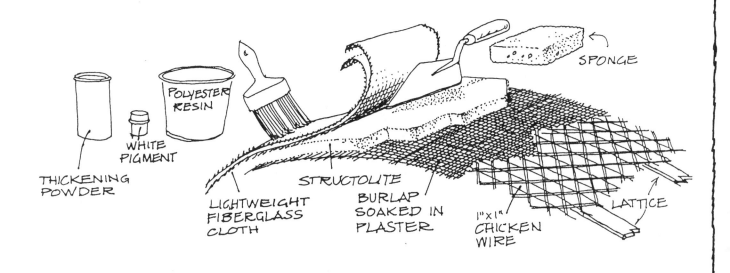

SPONGE

POLYESTER RESIN

WHITE PIGMENT

THICKENING POWDER

LIGHTWEIGHT FIBERGLASS CLOTH

STRUCTOLITE

BURLAP SOAKED IN PLASTER

1" x 1" CHICKEN WIRE

LATTICE

Ad Hoc Tree Fort

WIND VANE

OLD BEACH UMBRELLA

CROW'S NEST LOOKOUT TOWER

TIN CAN CHIMES

CLIMBING STEPS

PINWHEEL

BELL

CANVAS PUNCHING BAG FILLED WITH FOAM "PEANUTS"

CLIMBING STEPS

DART BOARD

TIRE SWING

TIRE INNER TUBE SEATING

This is a good project for kids to build themselves and allows their creativity to shine. Give them some leftover lumber, nails and a hammer and let them use their own imagination. Just make sure that all connections are safe, strong and secure. Quite often, discarded lumber can be found at the local dump after someone has demolished a deck. You can also use fallen trees from the woods. Just make sure that the wood is not rotten. Add a rope swing made from an old tire and tire inner tubes for seating underneath. Before you know it, you have a backyard clubhouse.

CONSTRUCTION TIPS

Beams can be attached (and removed) using "duplex" double-headed nails. To make it easier to remove them, first drill a 1/8-inch-diameter pilot hole in the beam (but not into the tree).

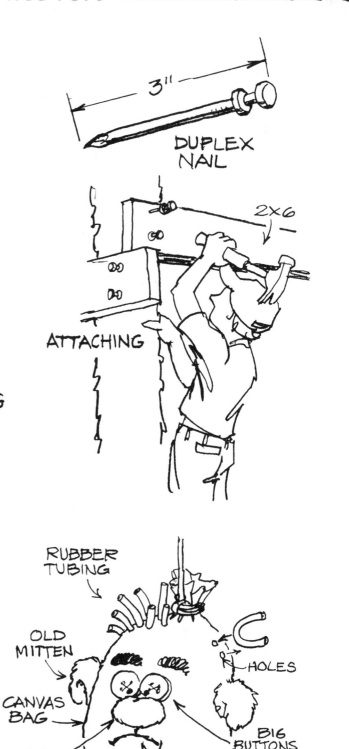

DUPLEX NAIL

3"

2X6

ATTACHING

24" WRECKING BAR

REMOVING

PUNCHING BAG

Find a canvas bag and fill it with plastic foam "peanuts." Tie it at the top with heavy string. Attach "hair" (foam or rubber tubing) by making 2 holes and inserting the tube into 1 hole and out the other.

RUBBER TUBING

OLD MITTEN

HOLES

CANVAS BAG

BIG BUTTONS

OLD SOCK STUFFED WITH COTTON

FOAM PEANUTS

PAINT OR BLACK THREAD

DELTA WING SPACE VEHICLE

The Delta Wing Space Vehicle is constructed from just 3 pieces of MDO plywood, a cardboard Sonatube, one 4 x 4-foot piece of Plexiglas and some 2x4s. To make the Delta wing, special order a 10-foot-long piece of 3/4-inch MDO plywood and cut it in half diagonally. The other 2 pieces of MDO plywood are a standard size 4x8 and are found at most local lumberyards. MDO plywood is often used for highway signs. It is an excellent material for outdoor projects and accepts paint well, unlike other plywood. Cut the 3-foot-long jet engines from a 9-inch-diameter cardboard Sonatube and paint them with an exterior varnish to resist weathering.

You can enter the playhouse by crawling through an opening underneath the wing. Copy an aeronautical gauge panel from the Internet and make it into an instrument panel for your space vehicle. Make the cockpit canopy out of 2 pieces of 1/4-inch acrylic Plexiglas cemented together at the top with special acrylic cement sold for this purpose. Screw the landing gears (legs) to the underside of the wings and support them with plywood braces (see illustration).

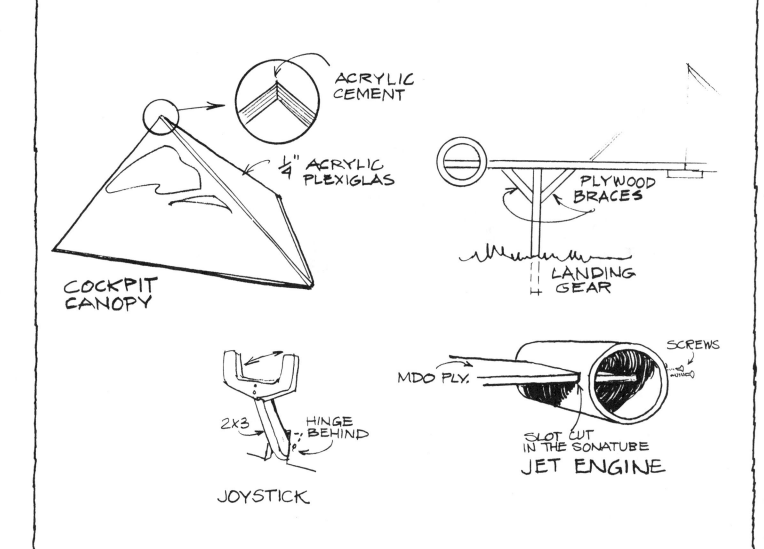

ACRYLIC CEMENT

1/4" ACRYLIC PLEXIGLAS

COCKPIT CANOPY

PLYWOOD BRACES

LANDING GEAR

2x3

HINGE BEHIND

JOYSTICK

MDO PLY.

SCREWS

SLOT CUT IN THE SONATUBE

JET ENGINE

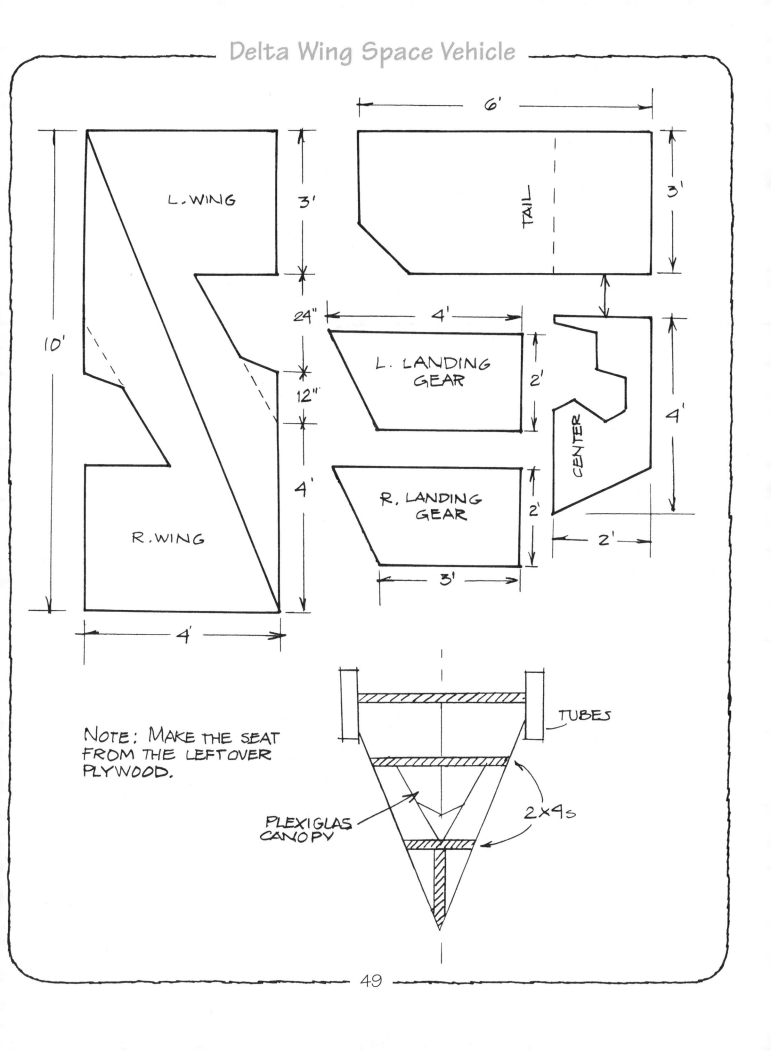

L. WING

3'

10'

24"

12"

4'

R. WING

4'

6'

TAIL

3'

4'

L. LANDING GEAR

2'

R. LANDING GEAR

2'

3'

CENTER

4'

2'

NOTE: MAKE THE SEAT FROM THE LEFTOVER PLYWOOD.

TUBES

2x4s

PLEXIGLAS CANOPY

Jet Racer

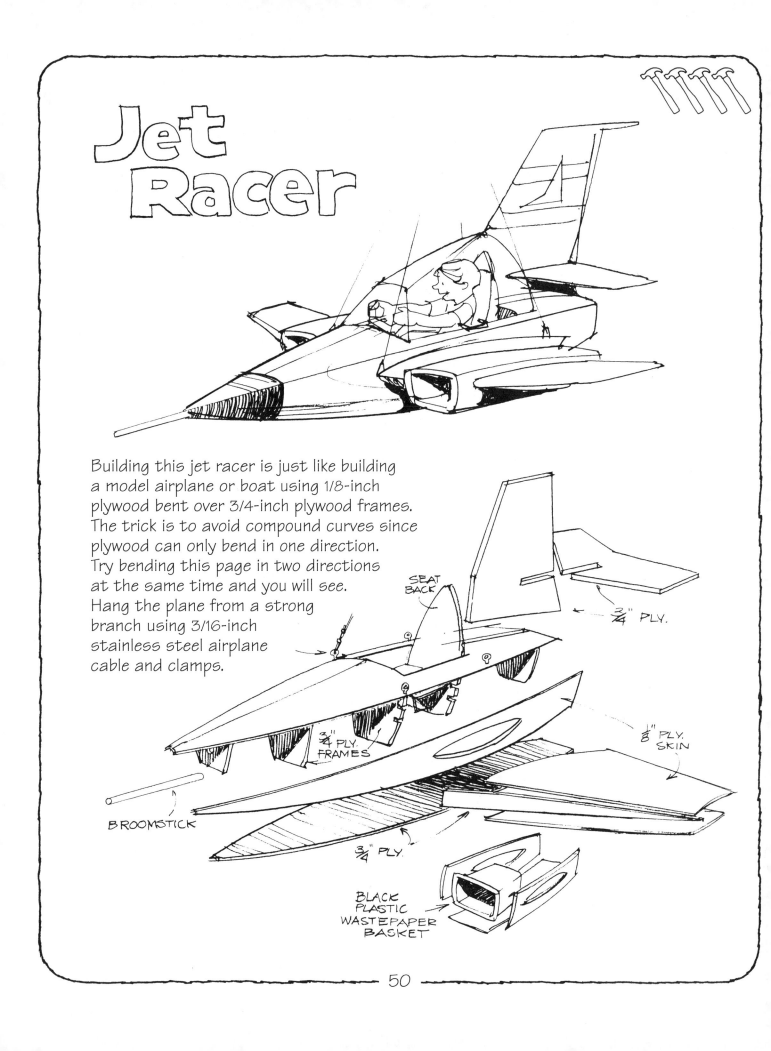

Building this jet racer is just like building a model airplane or boat using 1/8-inch plywood bent over 3/4-inch plywood frames. The trick is to avoid compound curves since plywood can only bend in one direction. Try bending this page in two directions at the same time and you will see. Hang the plane from a strong branch using 3/16-inch stainless steel airplane cable and clamps.

SEAT BACK

3/4" PLY.

3/4" PLY. FRAMES

BROOMSTICK

1/8" PLY. SKIN

3/4" PLY.

BLACK PLASTIC WASTEPAPER BASKET

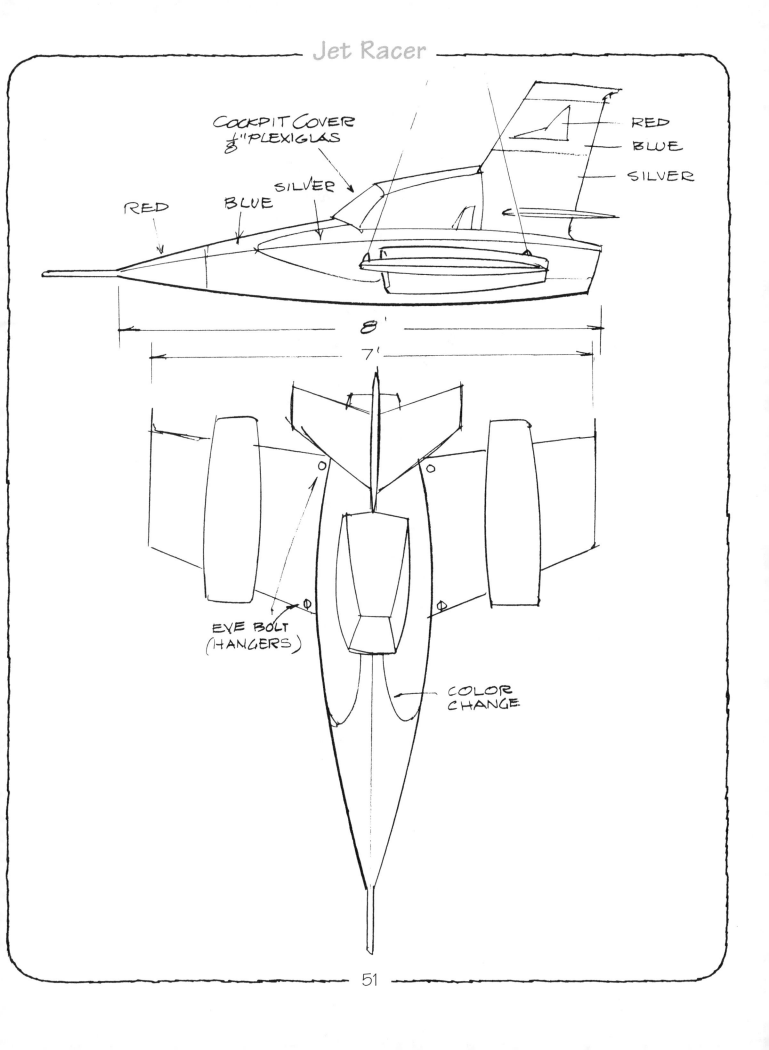

COCKPIT COVER
⅛" PLEXIGLAS

RED

BLUE

SILVER

RED

BLUE

SILVER

8'

7'

EYE BOLT
(HANGERS)

COLOR
CHANGE

KUNG FU HUT

We suggest building this meditation treehouse in a secluded spot, overlooking the water or with a spectacular view. It's a perfect place to meditate, practice yoga or just read a good book, undisturbed. It stands on top of a large sturdy tree stump. Choose a dead tree, with a trunk that has a wide circumference, and chainsaw the top so that it is level, approximately 8 to 10 feet from the ground. After you finish building the treehouse, access it with a removable ladder, hidden from view when you're not there, to discourage uninvited visitors. The side and back windows are circular, relating to the circular front door, and are covered with decorative grills. You can stucco the walls using Structolite. Camouflage the treehouse by adding colored paint powders to the stucco to make it a light grey-tan (see illustration).

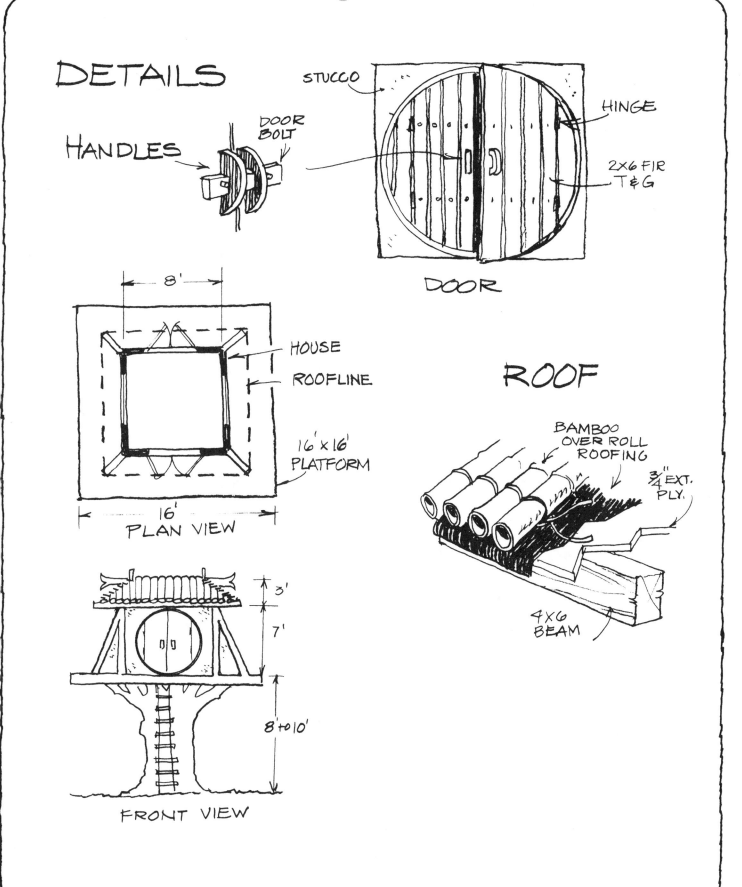

DETAILS

HANDLES

STUCCO

DOOR BOLT

HINGE

2X6 FIR T&G

DOOR

8'

HOUSE ROOFLINE

16' X 16' PLATFORM

16'

PLAN VIEW

ROOF

BAMBOO OVER ROLL ROOFING

3/4" EXT. PLY.

4X6 BEAM

3'

7'

8' to 10'

FRONT VIEW

Things That Move

Downhill Racer

This downhill racer is like a soapbox derby racer but much less expensive and easier to make. You can use wheels taken from an old baby carriage or stroller, or you can buy wheels for under $5 apiece (see **Resources**). The steering mechanism is made using inexpensive 1/2-inch (inside diameter) steel pipe fittings found in most hardware stores. The brakes are operated by a hinged brake pedal, which pulls a 1x4 brake board against the back wheels by means of light cable made from picture-hanging wire.

The seat rest and back support can be repositioned to suit the size of the driver by unscrewing five screws.

SIDE VIEW

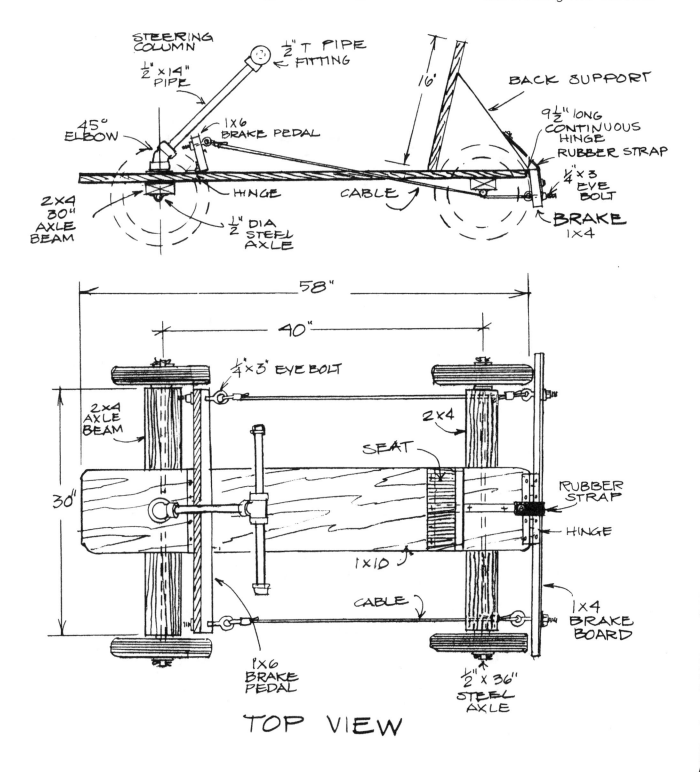

STEERING COLUMN

½" T PIPE FITTING

½" × 14" PIPE

BACK SUPPORT

16"

45° ELBOW

1×6 BRAKE PEDAL

9½" LONG CONTINUOUS HINGE

RUBBER STRAP

¼" × 3 EYE BOLT

2×4 30" AXLE BEAM

HINGE

CABLE

BRAKE 1×4

½" DIA STEEL AXLE

58"

40"

¼" × 3" EYE BOLT

2×4 AXLE BEAM

2×4

SEAT

RUBBER STRAP

30"

HINGE

1×10

CABLE

1×4 BRAKE BOARD

1×6 BRAKE PEDAL

½" × 36" STEEL AXLE

TOP VIEW

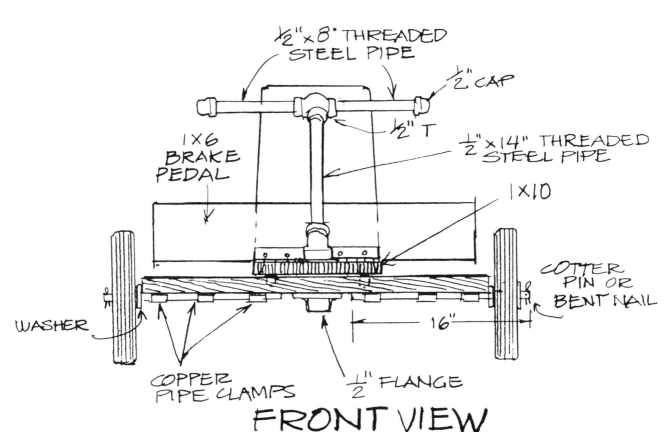

½"×8" THREADED STEEL PIPE

½" CAP

½" T

1×6 BRAKE PEDAL

½"×14" THREADED STEEL PIPE

1×10

COTTER PIN OR BENT NAIL

WASHER

16"

COPPER PIPE CLAMPS

½" FLANGE

FRONT VIEW

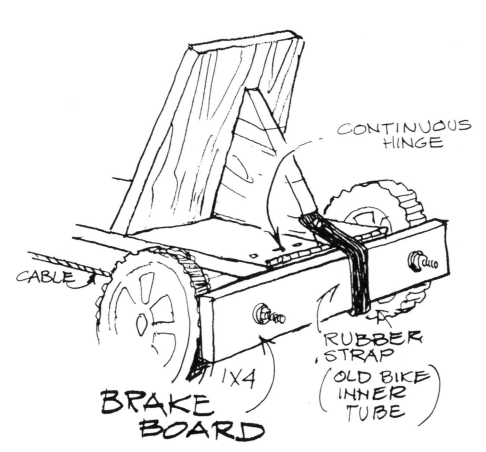

CONTINUOUS HINGE

CABLE

1×4

RUBBER STRAP (OLD BIKE INNER TUBE)

BRAKE BOARD

The rubber strap holds the brake board back, out of the way when freewheeling down the hill.

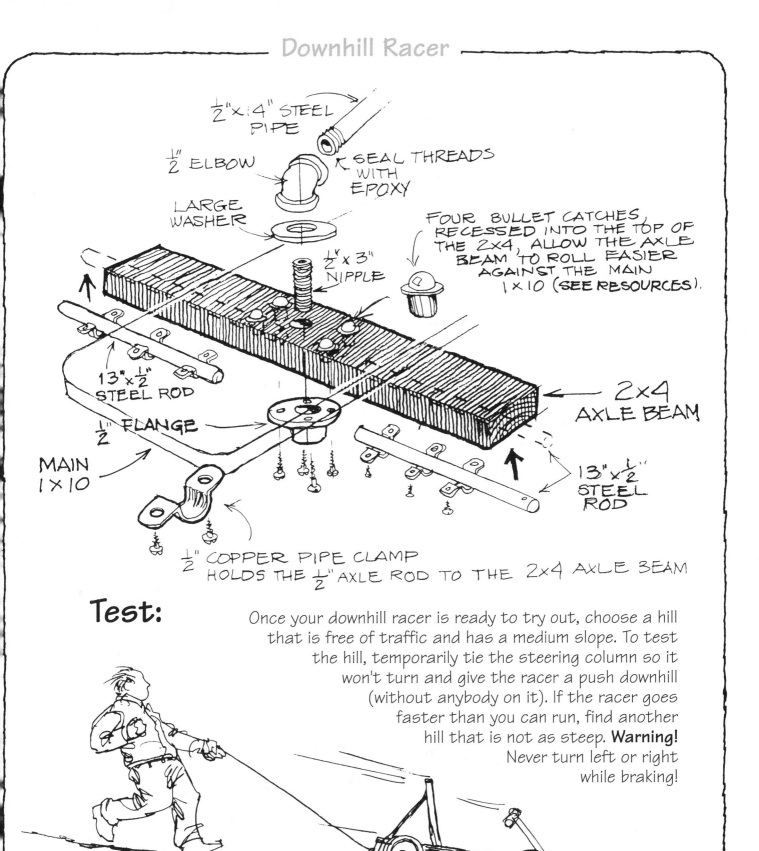

$\frac{1}{2}$" x 4" STEEL PIPE

$\frac{1}{2}$" ELBOW

SEAL THREADS WITH EPOXY

LARGE WASHER

FOUR BULLET CATCHES, RECESSED INTO THE TOP OF THE 2x4, ALLOW THE AXLE BEAM TO ROLL EASIER AGAINST THE MAIN 1x10 (SEE RESOURCES).

$\frac{1}{2}$" x 3" NIPPLE

2x4 AXLE BEAM

13" x $\frac{1}{2}$" STEEL ROD

$\frac{1}{2}$" FLANGE

MAIN 1x10

13" x $\frac{1}{2}$" STEEL ROD

$\frac{1}{2}$" COPPER PIPE CLAMP HOLDS THE $\frac{1}{2}$" AXLE ROD TO THE 2x4 AXLE BEAM

Test:

Once your downhill racer is ready to try out, choose a hill that is free of traffic and has a medium slope. To test the hill, temporarily tie the steering column so it won't turn and give the racer a push downhill (without anybody on it). If the racer goes faster than you can run, find another hill that is not as steep. **Warning!** Never turn left or right while braking!

TIP:
CHECK OUT THE WILDEST SOAP BOX DERBY RACE AT WWW.REDBULLSOAPBOXUSA.COM.

EMBELLISH YOUR DOWNHILL RACER TO
MAKE IT UNIQUE.

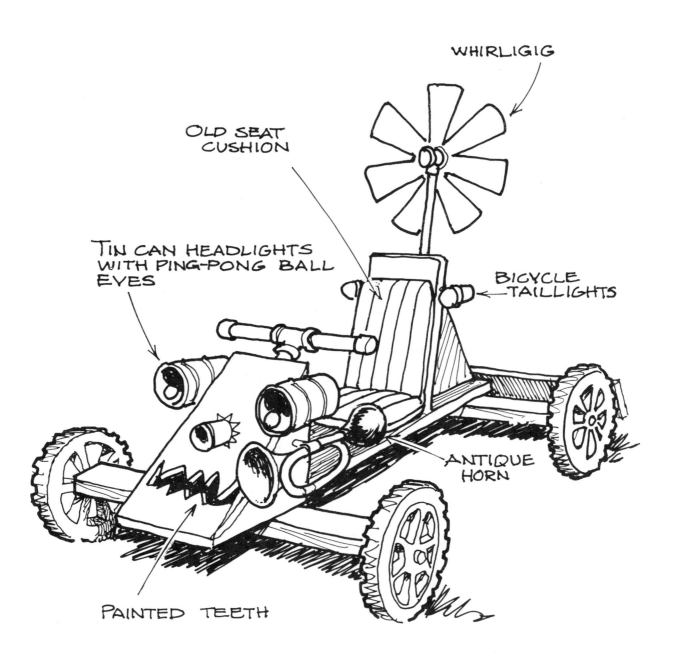

WHIRLIGIG

OLD SEAT
CUSHION

TIN CAN HEADLIGHTS
WITH PING-PONG BALL
EYES

BICYCLE
TAILLIGHTS

ANTIQUE
HORN

PAINTED TEETH

Ski Sled

Wait! Don't throw
out that old pair of skis!
Make a ski sled out of them
instead. The ski sled shown here holds
3 to 4 people. It is better than a regular sled
because it can slide over unpacked snow, whereas a
regular sled's thin steel runners need packed snow on which
to slide. We also prefer it to a toboggan because it has a backrest for mom and a
place for dad to stand in the back. You can steer it by shifting your weight from
one side to the other. All you need (besides the skis) to make this ski sled are a
few pieces of plywood and some inexpensive pipe fittings.

Making the Sled

Remove the bindings from the skis using a hammer and a heavy-duty screwdriver.

Cut a piece of 3/4-inch plywood 16 inches wide and 6 inches less than the length of the skis.

24"
16"
HANDLE
1 3/8" DIA. POLE
BACK-REST
20"
12°
3/4" PLYWOOD
BACK SUPPORT
21"
8"
FOOT-REST
16"
1/2" PIPE CROSSBARS
6" LESS THAN LENGTH OF SKIS
10"

6"
12°   12°
20"
BACK SUPPORT
12"

Cut the bottom edge of the backrest at a 12-degree angle and screw it to the sled from underneath. Screw on the back support as well.

Assemble the 2 crossbars. Coat the pipe threads with epoxy. Attach them to the skis using 1/2-inch pipe flanges and 3/16 x 7/8-inch flat-head bolts. Attach the crossbars to the underside of the sled using 5 copper pipe brackets on each crossbar.

24"
CROSSBAR 1/2" i.d. PIPE

1/2" x 6" PIPE
PIPE FLANGE
SKI
3/16" x 7/8" BOLT
COUNTERSINK BOLTS
SECTION VIEW

COPPER PIPE BRACKET
FLANGE

Note: i.d. = inside dimension

Box Sled

This sled is easy to make and requires only an old wine box and some 1x6 boards. It is perfect for towing a young child over packed snow. You can also use it to haul firewood or bring home groceries after an ice storm.

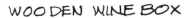

WOODEN WINE BOX

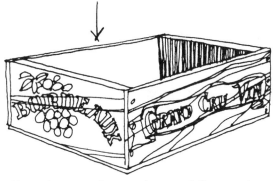

Knock out the end panel from the piece that you just sawed off. Use this for the front of the sled, nailing the sides to it.

Begin by sawing off one end of the box at a 35-degree angle.

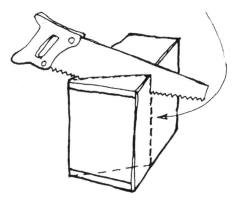

Nail the sides to the end panel (the front of the sled). Then nail two 1x6 angled boards to the sides, turning it into a sled.

END PANEL BECOMES FRONT OF SLED

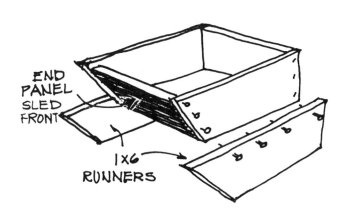

END PANEL SLED FRONT

1X6 RUNNERS

SEESAW

This is a takeoff of the traditional seesaw from yesteryear. As you rock back and forth, a 4-foot propeller rotates by means of ropes attached to the seesaw beam. This seesaw can be built in a weekend and requires only a few pieces of lumber.

You will need:

- (2) pieces of pressure-treated (p.t.) 2x8s, 10 feet long

- (1) 2x8, 8 feet long for the spacer between the posts

- (1) 2x8, 12 feet long for the seesaw beam and seat

- (1) piece of 3/4-inch exterior plywood, 48 x 48 inches for the propeller

Embed the post 3 feet into the ground and cast a 2-foot-diameter concrete collar around it.

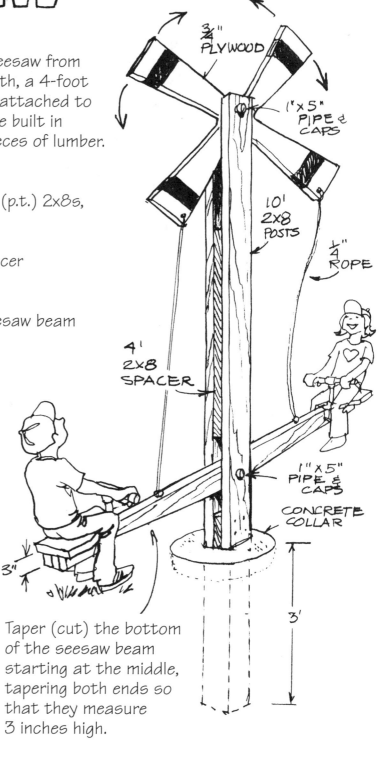

Taper (cut) the bottom of the seesaw beam starting at the middle, tapering both ends so that they measure 3 inches high.

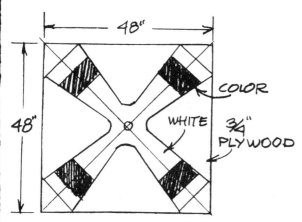

PROPELLER

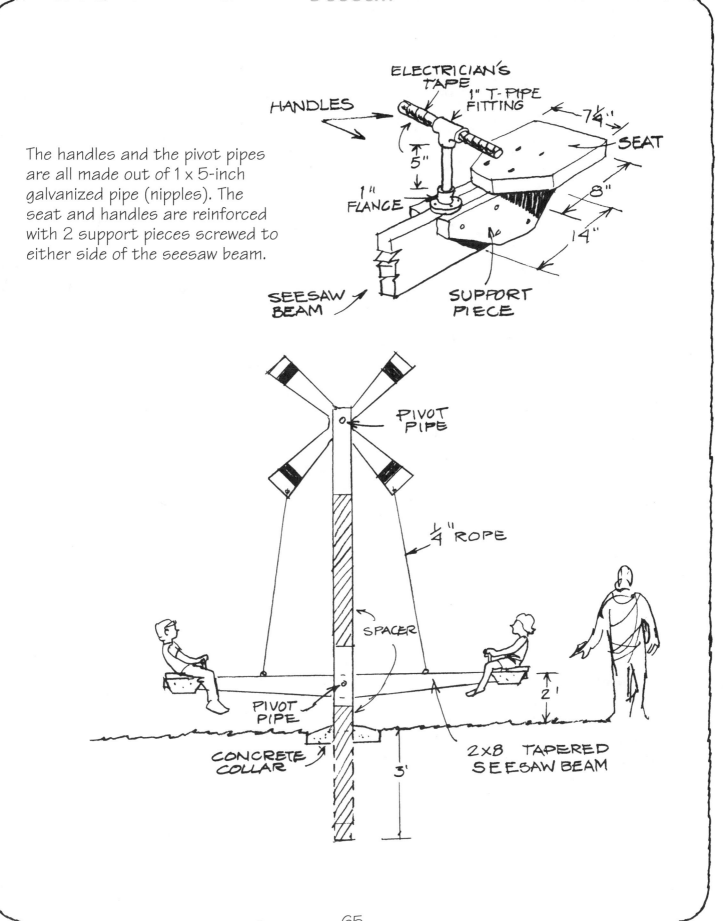

ELECTRICIAN'S
TAPE

1" T-PIPE
FITTING

HANDLES

7¼"

SEAT

5"

8"

1"
FLANGE

14"

The handles and the pivot pipes
are all made out of 1 x 5-inch
galvanized pipe (nipples). The
seat and handles are reinforced
with 2 support pieces screwed to
either side of the seesaw beam.

SEESAW
BEAM

SUPPORT
PIECE

PIVOT
PIPE

¼" ROPE

SPACER

2'

PIVOT
PIPE

CONCRETE
COLLAR

2x8 TAPERED
SEESAW BEAM

3'

Trolley Ride

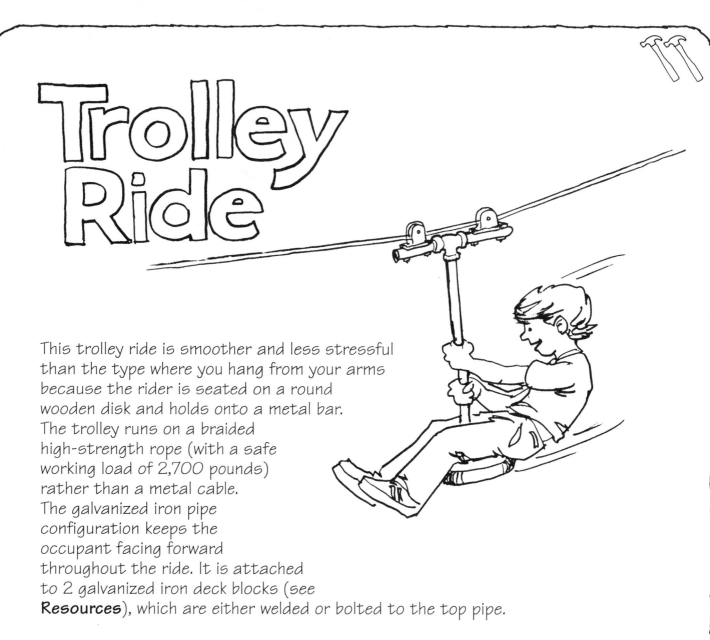

This trolley ride is smoother and less stressful than the type where you hang from your arms because the rider is seated on a round wooden disk and holds onto a metal bar. The trolley runs on a braided high-strength rope (with a safe working load of 2,700 pounds) rather than a metal cable. The galvanized iron pipe configuration keeps the occupant facing forward throughout the ride. It is attached to 2 galvanized iron deck blocks (see **Resources**), which are either welded or bolted to the top pipe.

Choose 2 sturdy trees that are at least 10 inches in diameter (so they don't bend) and about 50 to 75 feet apart. Clear the area between the trees from any rocks or branches that could be in the way. The starting point for the trolley ride should be higher than the destination point. A good rule of thumb is to make the starting point 6 inches higher for every 10 feet of length and then make adjustments as necessary. Remember to deduct the slope of the land if the destination tree is downhill from the starting tree. Also, you should design it so that there is a rise to the rope at the end to slow down the rider before you reach the second tree.

Making the Trolley

Attach deck blocks by drilling 2 bolt holes in each 4-inch-long galvanized pipe (nipple) and bolting them on. Use a drill press to make the holes or have a metal shop weld the blocks onto the pipe.

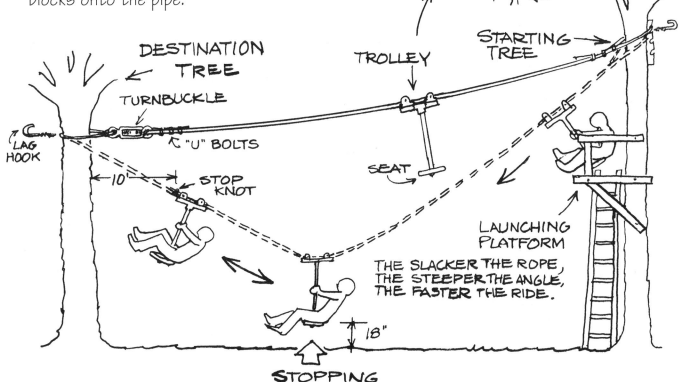

GALV. DECK BLOCKS
(SEE RESOURCES)

½" ROPE

4" GALV. NIPPLE

1" Tee

BOLT

1" x 36" GALV. PIPE

STARTING TREE

TROLLEY

DESTINATION TREE

TURNBUCKLE

LAG HOOK

"U" BOLTS

10'

STOP KNOT

SEAT

LAUNCHING PLATFORM

THE SLACKER THE ROPE, THE STEEPER THE ANGLE, THE FASTER THE RIDE.

18"

STOPPING POINT

Setting Up the Line

Start by temporarily tying a rope 8 to 10 feet high in the "destination" tree. Place the trolley on the rope and then tie the rope to the "starting" tree. Make the rope as tight as possible by using a turnbuckle (see **Resources**). Test the trolley by attaching 2 or 3 concrete blocks (about 30 pounds each) to approximate the weight of a child and allowing it to ride down the rope and partway back until it stops. It should end up being about 18 inches off the ground. Raise or lower the rope on the "starting" tree until it is just right. Once you are satisfied, screw a forged lag hook (see **Resources**) permanently into the destination tree to hold the rope. Secure both ends of the rope with 3 U-bolts. To stop the rider from crashing into the tree, tie a stop knot 10 feet in front of the destination tree.

To allow for adjustments and to protect the cambium layer of the starting tree, make 2 notched 2x4 bars to hold the rope in place.

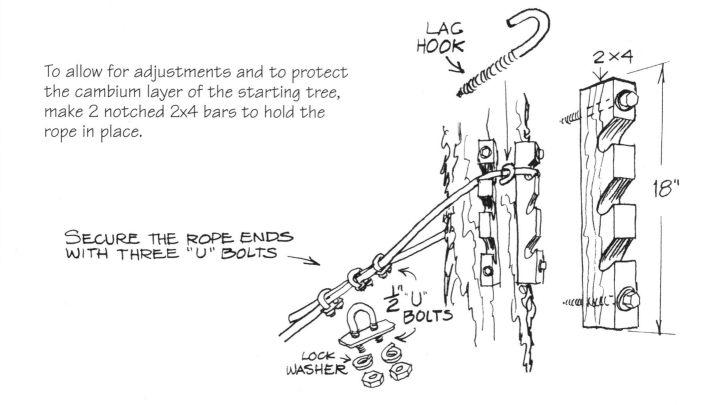

LAG HOOK

2×4

18"

SECURE THE ROPE ENDS WITH THREE "U" BOLTS

$\frac{1}{2}$" U BOLTS

LOCK WASHER

Depending on your situation, you may need to build some sort of launching platform at the "starting" tree. A treehouse would be ideal, but a simple tree stand works as well.

TREE STAND

Safety Tips

Since safety is a major concern, make sure that an adult supervises each rider by running alongside for the first few times. During each descent, instruct the rider to shout out "CLEAR THE WAY" before launching. The rope specified here should last many years, but for safety reasons, it should still be checked every year for abrasion.

Circle Swing

This swing should take only a few hours to build. It is made by cutting two 4-foot-diameter circles from a single sheet of 3/4-inch-thick plywood, glued and screwed together. Use 3/4-inch-diameter braided rope to secure it to a high, overhanging tree branch. The seat should be 12 to 16 inches off the ground (depending on the size of the kids using it). To cover the edge of the plywood, use an old hose, cut lengthwise and nailed to the edge.

OLD HOSE

(2) 4'-DIAMETER CIRCLES GLUED TOGETHER

CREDIT: J.C. STILES

Merry-Go-Round

ENLARGED DETAIL

GUNWALE EDGING (SEE RESOURCES)

This backyard merry-go-round is made from a single sheet of 3/4-inch plywood and a cable spool that is used by the telephone company to store wire (cable used to run lines from pole to pole). Since the spools can vary in size, it is impossible to give exact dimensions; however, the following directions should serve as a useful guide.

If the telephone spool is too tall for your kids to play on, you can bury the bottom half of the spool in the ground. As an extra precaution to keep it from moving, secure it in the ground with six or seven 1/2-inch-diameter, 10-inch-long anchor bolts, set in concrete.

Make the top disk out of two 48-inch-square pieces of 3/4-inch plywood, cut into a circle and glued and screwed together. Cover the edge of the disks with vinyl marine gunwale (gunnel) edging or an old garden hose, cut lengthwise down the middle.

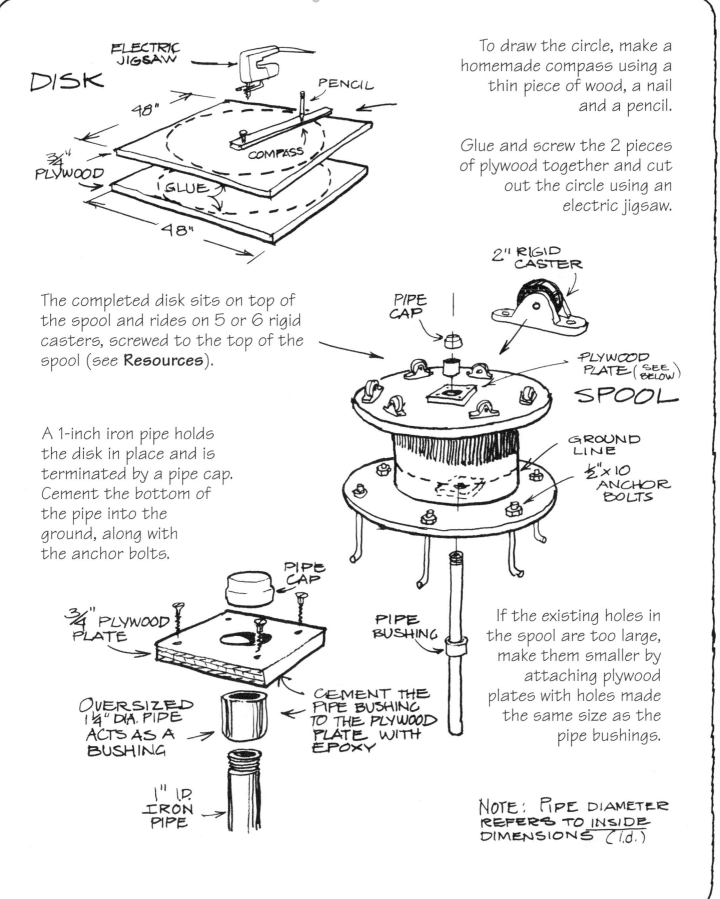

DISK

ELECTRIC JIGSAW

PENCIL

48"

3/4" PLYWOOD

COMPASS

GLUE

48"

To draw the circle, make a homemade compass using a thin piece of wood, a nail and a pencil.

Glue and screw the 2 pieces of plywood together and cut out the circle using an electric jigsaw.

The completed disk sits on top of the spool and rides on 5 or 6 rigid casters, screwed to the top of the spool (see **Resources**).

PIPE CAP

2" RIGID CASTER

PLYWOOD PLATE (SEE BELOW)

SPOOL

A 1-inch iron pipe holds the disk in place and is terminated by a pipe cap. Cement the bottom of the pipe into the ground, along with the anchor bolts.

GROUND LINE

1/2" x 10 ANCHOR BOLTS

PIPE CAP

3/4" PLYWOOD PLATE

PIPE BUSHING

OVERSIZED 1 1/4" DIA. PIPE ACTS AS A BUSHING

CEMENT THE PIPE BUSHING TO THE PLYWOOD PLATE WITH EPOXY

1" I.D. IRON PIPE

If the existing holes in the spool are too large, make them smaller by attaching plywood plates with holes made the same size as the pipe bushings.

NOTE: PIPE DIAMETER REFERS TO INSIDE DIMENSIONS (I.D.)

Model Sailboat

What to do on a rainy day? Build a model sailboat for a sunny day! This 18-inch sailboat may take more than a day to build, but you will have fun building it and even more fun sailing it. Don't worry about the boat sinking; it's made of unsinkable Styrofoam that is easy to carve and shape. All you need is a piece of Styrofoam, found at most lumberyards.
Tip: They often have broken pieces they will give you for free.

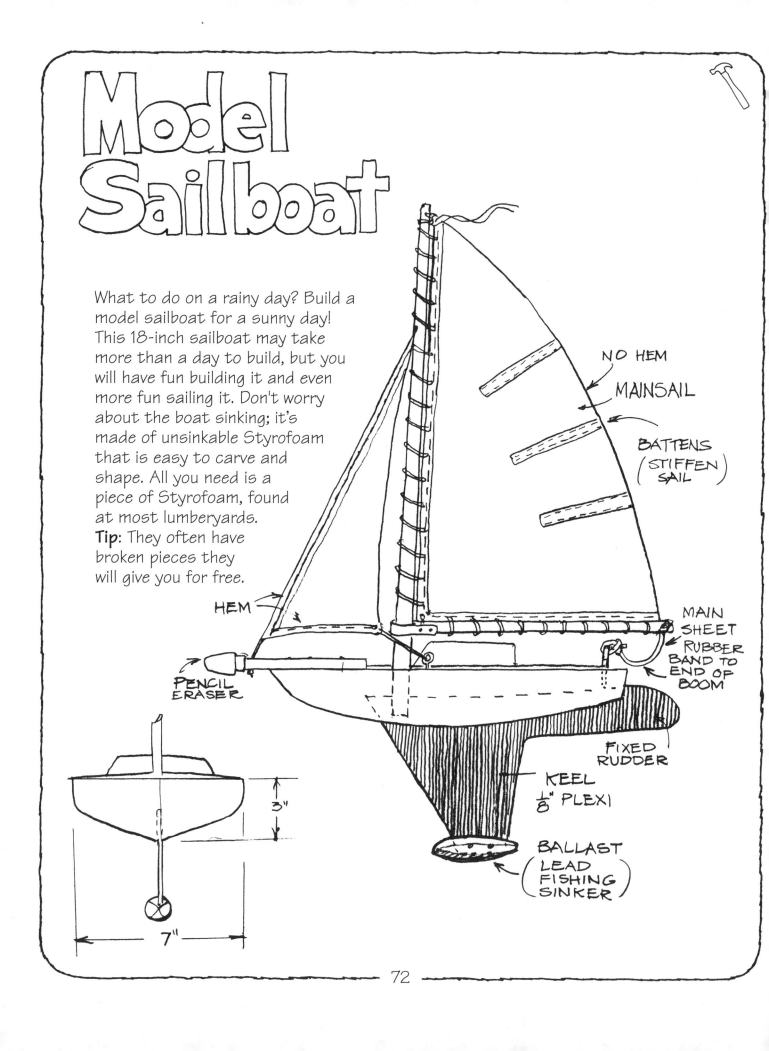

NO HEM

MAINSAIL

BATTENS
(STIFFEN SAIL)

HEM

PENCIL ERASER

MAIN SHEET RUBBER BAND TO END OF BOOM

FIXED RUDDER

KEEL
$\frac{1}{8}$" PLEXI

BALLAST
(LEAD FISHING SINKER)

3"

7"

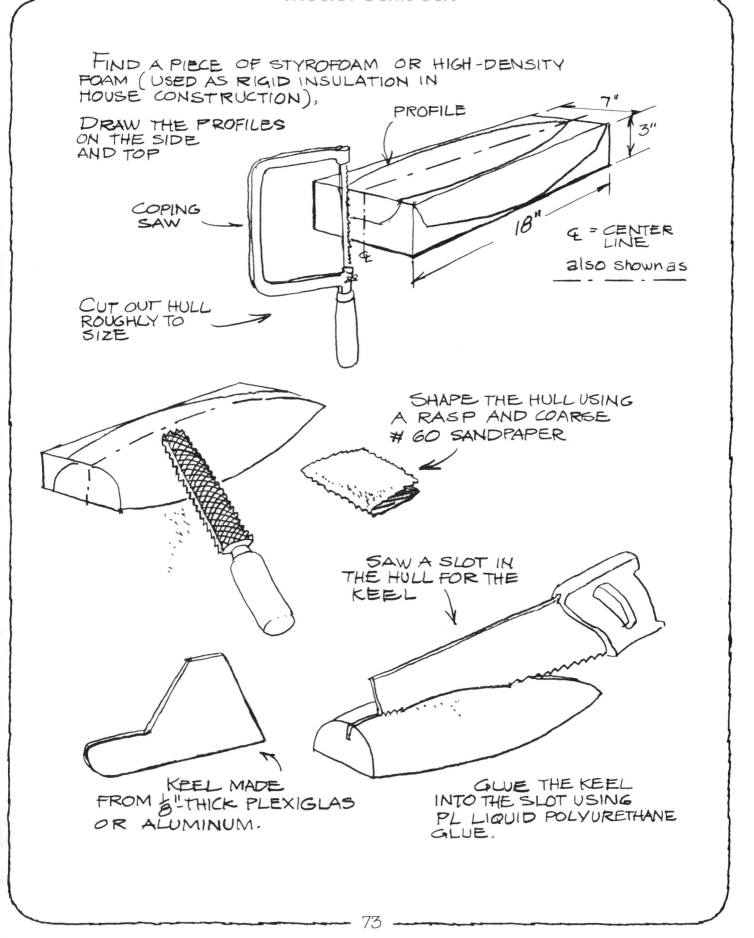

FIND A PIECE OF STYROFOAM OR HIGH-DENSITY FOAM (USED AS RIGID INSULATION IN HOUSE CONSTRUCTION).

DRAW THE PROFILES ON THE SIDE AND TOP

PROFILE

7"

3"

18"

$\mathcal{C}$ = CENTER LINE

also shown as

COPING SAW

CUT OUT HULL ROUGHLY TO SIZE

SHAPE THE HULL USING A RASP AND COARSE # 60 SANDPAPER

SAW A SLOT IN THE HULL FOR THE KEEL

KEEL MADE FROM $\frac{1}{8}$" THICK PLEXIGLAS OR ALUMINUM.

GLUE THE KEEL INTO THE SLOT USING PL LIQUID POLYURETHANE GLUE.

COVER THE HULL WITH POWDERED WATER PUTTY. (SEE RESOURCES) ONCE IT HAS HARDENED (ABOUT 45 MINS.), SAND IT SMOOTH.

USING A HAND SAW, CUT A SLOT IN A LEAD FISHING SINKER AND ATTACH IT TO THE KEEL WITH 2 SMALL BRASS NAILS.

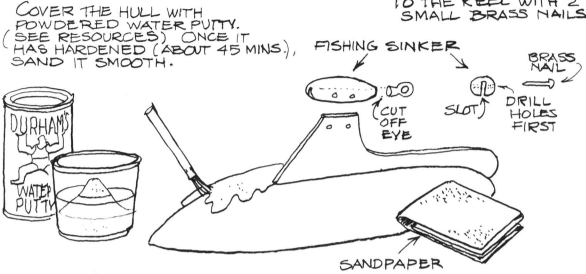

FISHING SINKER

BRASS NAIL

CUT OFF EYE

SLOT

DRILL HOLES FIRST

DURHAM'S WATER PUTTY

SANDPAPER

TURN THE BOAT OVER TO THE TOPSIDE.

TIP: IT IS A GOOD IDEA TO MAKE A STAND FOR THE BOAT. YOU WILL NEED ONE LATER ON, AND IT MAKES IT EASIER TO BUILD THE RIGGING, ETC.

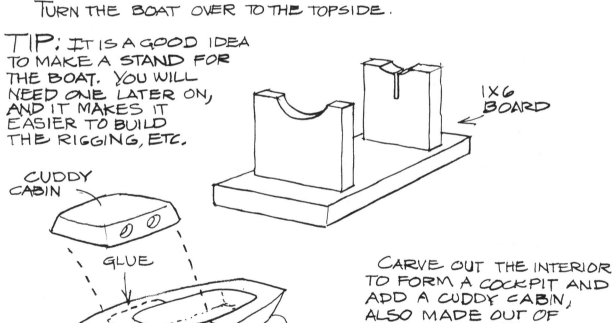

1X6 BOARD

CUDDY CABIN

GLUE

CARVE OUT THE INTERIOR TO FORM A COCKPIT AND ADD A CUDDY CABIN, ALSO MADE OUT OF STYROFOAM. THEN COVER THE TOPSIDE WITH WATER PUTTY, THE SAME AS THE BOTTOM.

DETAILS

Step the mast by drilling a 3/8-inch-diameter hole in the deck and inserting a 3/8 x 18-inch-long dowel into it.

Attach the 3/8 x 17-inch-long boom to the mast by cutting and bending a piece of metal or plastic, wrapping it around the boom and attaching it to the mast with brass nails, clinched over on the opposite side.

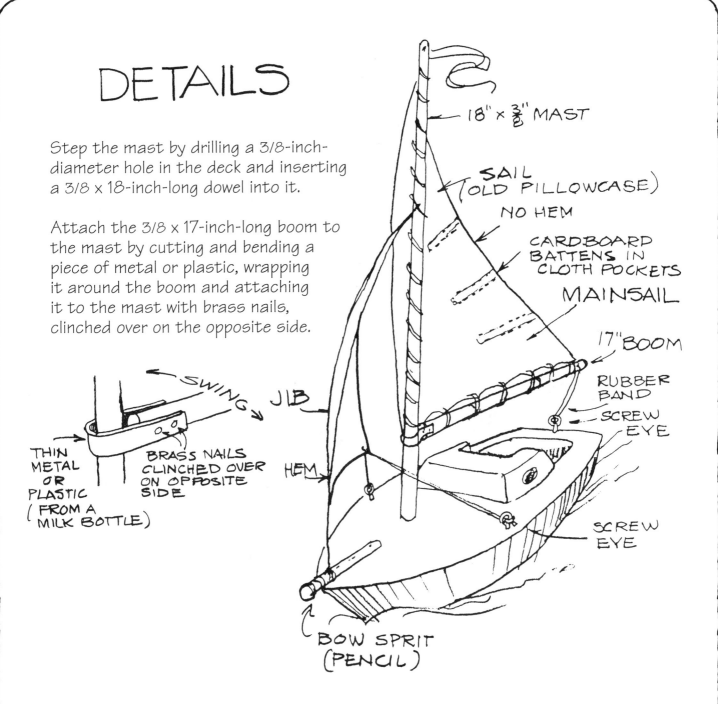

18" x 3/8" MAST

SAIL (OLD PILLOWCASE)

NO HEM

CARDBOARD BATTENS IN CLOTH POCKETS

MAINSAIL

17" BOOM

RUBBER BAND

SCREW EYE

SCREW EYE

SWING

JIB

HEM

THIN METAL OR PLASTIC (FROM A MILK BOTTLE)

BRASS NAILS CLINCHED OVER ON OPPOSITE SIDE

BOW SPRIT (PENCIL)

Cut the sails from an old pillowcase or bedsheet. Using a sewing machine, hem the forward and bottom sides of the 2 sails, but not the back sides. To stiffen the mainsail, add cardboard battens, sewn into the back side of the sail. To hold the boom to the boat, tie a 6-inch-long piece of rubber band to a screw eye on the stern (back) of the boat. Its purpose is to prevent the boat from capsizing with a sudden gust of wind. It will need adjusting to get it right.

Recycled Raft

If you save a 1-gallon plastic milk or water carton every day for 4 1/4 months, you will have enough cartons to build this inexpensive raft. In addition, you will need one 4x8 sheet of 3/4-inch-thick plywood, five 1x12 boards, some chicken wire, and two 1x4s for the skids underneath. Since each carton is an independent float, if one breaks, the raft will still float. You can build this raft in just a few hours.

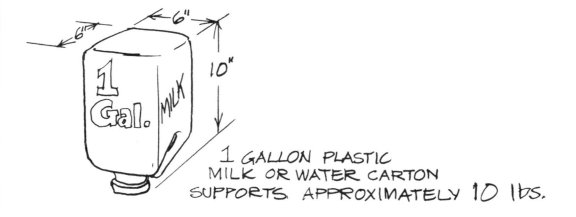

1 GALLON PLASTIC
MILK OR WATER CARTON
SUPPORTS APPROXIMATELY 10 lbs.

FRAME

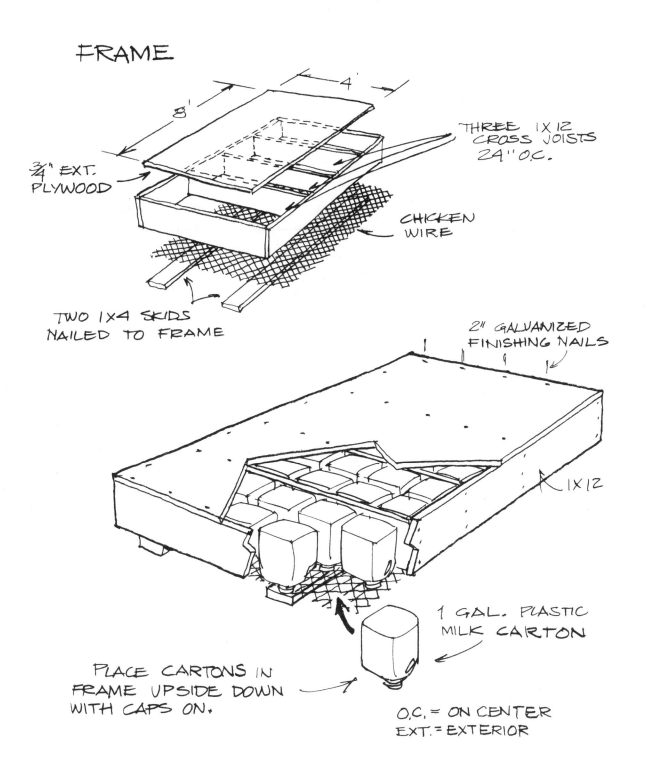

8'

4'

THREE 1X12 CROSS JOISTS 24" O.C.

3/4" EXT. PLYWOOD

CHICKEN WIRE

TWO 1X4 SKIDS NAILED TO FRAME

2" GALVANIZED FINISHING NAILS

1X12

1 GAL. PLASTIC MILK CARTON

PLACE CARTONS IN FRAME UPSIDE DOWN WITH CAPS ON.

O.C. = ON CENTER
EXT. = EXTERIOR

Pogo Boat

This is an easy
boat to build
because it has
no curved parts.
It will support 2 people
and is great for fishing or just
hanging out on the water. It fits easily on
top of a car in case you don't live near the water.

You will need:
- Two 1x12 cedar boards (with no knots), 8 feet long, for the sides.
- One 4x8 sheet of 1/4-inch plywood for the bottom.
- One 1x6, 6 feet long, for the ends.
- One 1x10 cedar board for the seats.
- Two 1x2s, 10 feet long, for the skids and seat supports.
- Waterproof glue and some screws and nails.

You can make your own oars out of leftover plywood, but you will have to buy the oarlocks (see **Resources**).

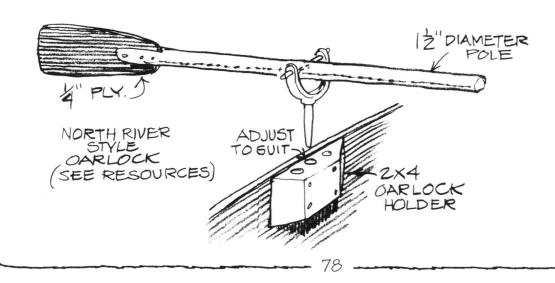

1½" DIAMETER POLE

¼" PLY.

NORTH RIVER STYLE OARLOCK (SEE RESOURCES)

ADJUST TO SUIT

2X4 OARLOCK HOLDER

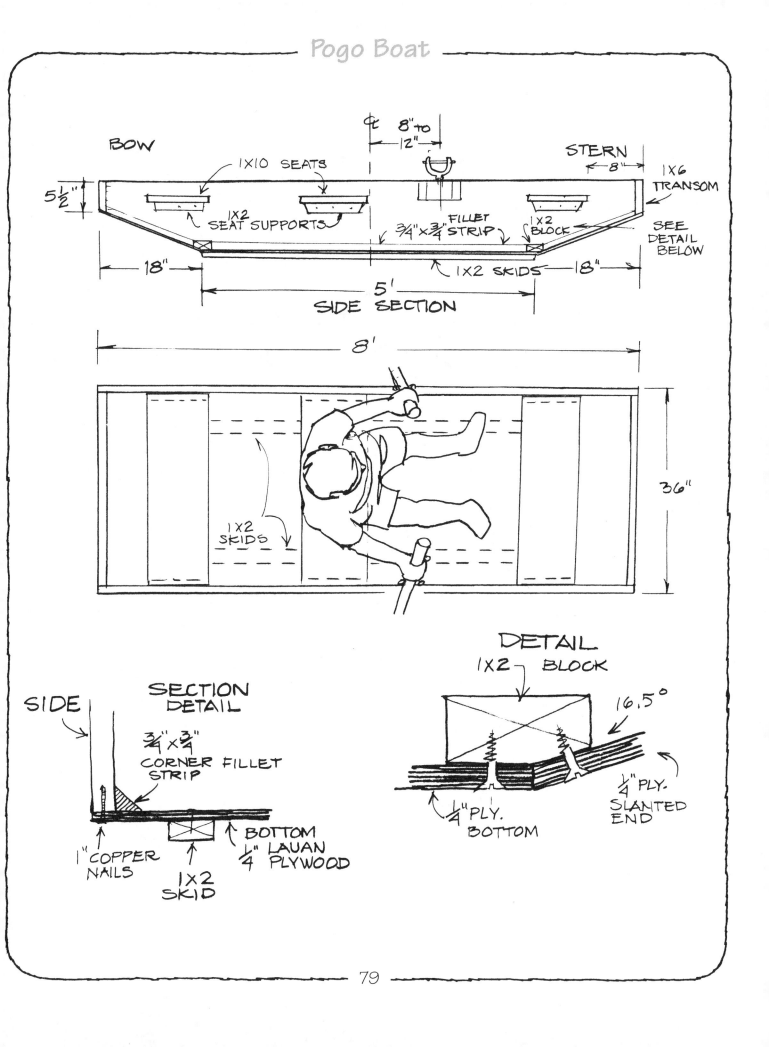

BOW

STERN

8" to 12"

1X10 SEATS

1X2 SEAT SUPPORTS

5½"

3/4" X 3/4" FILLET STRIP

1X2 BLOCK

1X6 TRANSOM

SEE DETAIL BELOW

18"

1X2 SKIDS

18"

5'

SIDE SECTION

8'

1X2 SKIDS

36"

SECTION DETAIL

SIDE

3/4" X 3/4" CORNER FILLET STRIP

1" COPPER NAILS

1X2 SKID

BOTTOM ¼" LAUAN PLYWOOD

DETAIL

1X2 BLOCK

16.5°

¼" PLY. BOTTOM

¼" PLY. SLANTED END

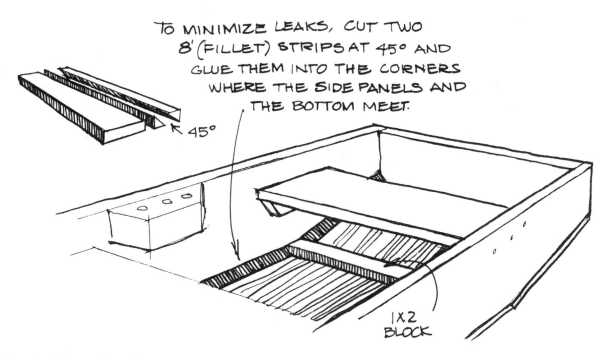

TO MINIMIZE LEAKS, CUT TWO 8' (FILLET) STRIPS AT 45° AND GLUE THEM INTO THE CORNERS WHERE THE SIDE PANELS AND THE BOTTOM MEET.

45°

1x2 BLOCK

Building the Boat

Cut the 8-foot sideboards so they slant down 18 inches from the ends. Glue and nail the sideboards to the transom ends.

Glue and nail the 1/4-inch plywood bottom to the sideboards.

Glue and nail the 1/4-inch plywood slanted bottom ends to the sideboards and transom ends.

To protect against leaks, cut, glue and screw two 1x2s where the bottom pieces of plywood join together. This requires shaving 1/4 inch off the bottom edges of the 1x2s to match the angle of the 2 plywood pieces.

Cut two 3/4 x 3/4-inch fillet strips, approximately 9 feet long, at a 45-degree angle. Glue them in the corners between the side panels and the bottom (see **Side Section**).

Install the 1x10 seats using 1x2 support cleats.

Cut and install the two 2x4 oarlock holders.

Screw (from the inside) two 1x2 skids to the bottom of the boat.
Note: For other dinghy plans, see **Resources**.

A-Frame Treehouse   81

Tree Fort

Above: Treasure Chest

Below: Downhill Racer

Kids, Build This First Sawhorse   84

Fake Barbells

Lemonade Stand

The Ugliest, Best, Cheapest Des

Exploding Cannon

Treehouse
Accessories

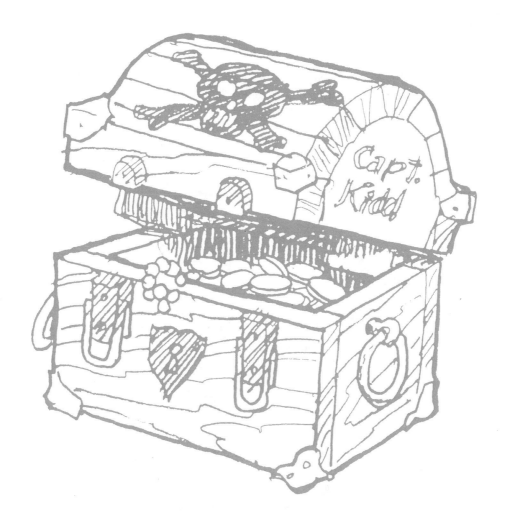

Treasure Chest...

...WITH A SECRET LOCK

This treasure chest has a secret lock that only you and
your friends will know how to open. It is fairly simple to build;
however, you will need an adult to bevel the top pieces on a table saw.
The secret to unlocking the treasure chest is in the 2 iron handles (see
Resources) on the sides that have to be turned counterclockwise several
times to unlock the top.

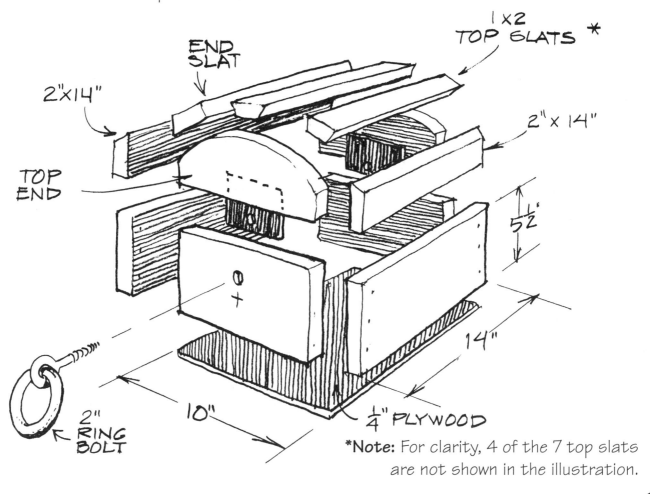

END
SLAT

1 x 2
TOP SLATS *

2"x14"

2" x 14"

TOP
END

$5\frac{1}{2}$"

14"

2"
RING
BOLT

10"

$\frac{1}{4}$" PLYWOOD

*Note: For clarity, 4 of the 7 top slats
are not shown in the illustration.

Making the Chest

Start by making a 10 x 14-inch box with a 1/4-inch-thick plywood bottom. Cut the top end pieces, using an electric jigsaw, at a 5 1/2-inch radius (see **Section View**). Bevel at 20 degrees the top edges of the two 2 x 14-inch front and back pieces. Bevel five 1x2 top slats at 7 1/2 degrees on both edges so that they fit together neatly. Cut 2 end slats to measure 1 3/4 inches wide x 14 inches long. Bevel one edge of each end slat at 45 degrees to fit the front and the back.

Install 2 trunk catches and a key plate to make it appear that a key is necessary to open the chest.

Glue and nail a 2 x 4-inch piece of 1/4-inch plywood to the top inside of each side of the chest. Close the chest and drill a hole through the outside of the chest and the inside flap. Screw the ring bolt into the sides and flaps to lock the chest.

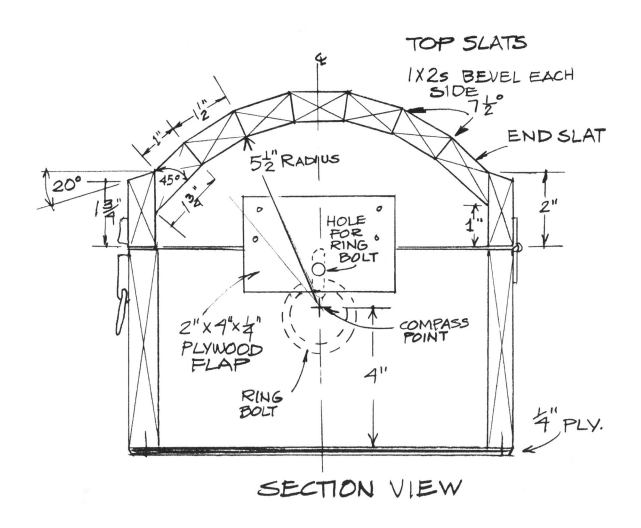

SECTION VIEW

Winch

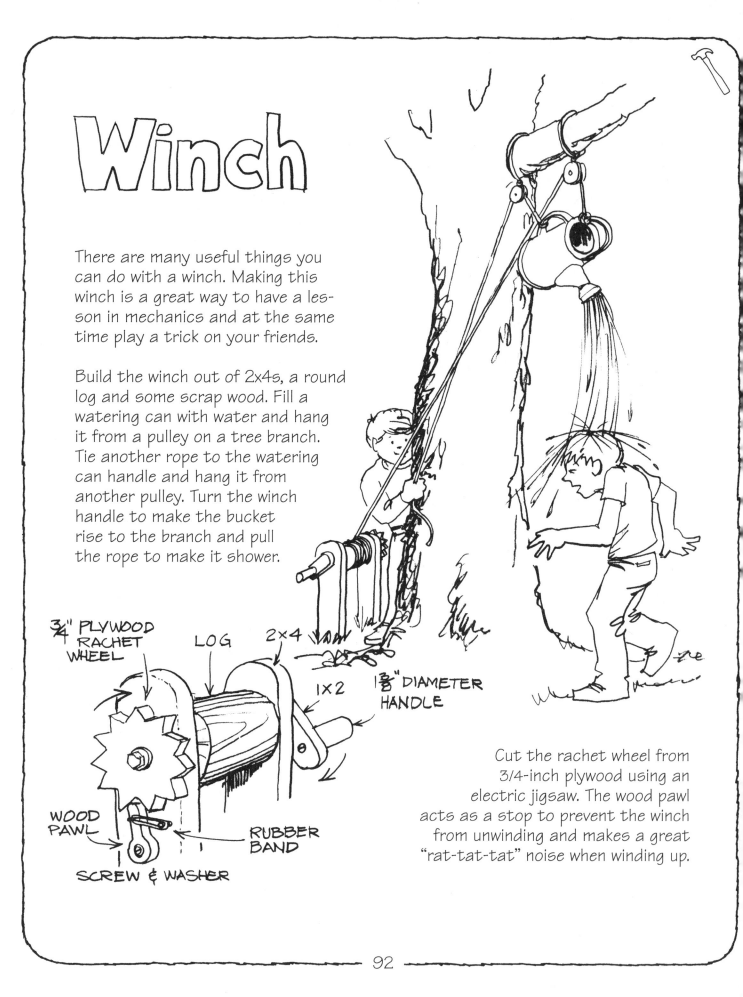

There are many useful things you can do with a winch. Making this winch is a great way to have a lesson in mechanics and at the same time play a trick on your friends.

Build the winch out of 2x4s, a round log and some scrap wood. Fill a watering can with water and hang it from a pulley on a tree branch. Tie another rope to the watering can handle and hang it from another pulley. Turn the winch handle to make the bucket rise to the branch and pull the rope to make it shower.

3/4" PLYWOOD RACHET WHEEL

LOG

2×4

1×2

1⅜" DIAMETER HANDLE

WOOD PAWL

RUBBER BAND

SCREW & WASHER

Cut the rachet wheel from 3/4-inch plywood using an electric jigsaw. The wood pawl acts as a stop to prevent the winch from unwinding and makes a great "rat-tat-tat" noise when winding up.

 # LOCKS and LATCHES

PULL DOWN HANDLE TO OPEN.

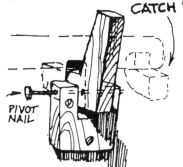

CATCH

PIVOT NAIL

This type of latch can be opened from both sides of the door. When properly constructed, a latch like this will lock shut when the wind blows the door closed.

Hidden Lock

Pulling an inconspicuous rope from the outside can open the door.

BAR A

B

Note: View shown here is from the inside of the house.

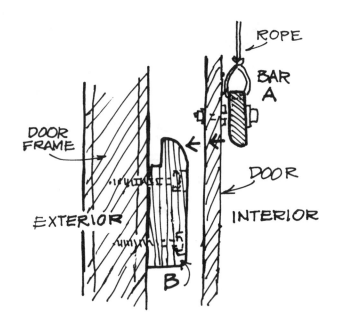

ROPE

BAR A

DOOR FRAME

DOOR

EXTERIOR

INTERIOR

B

COMBINATION LOCKS
REQUIRE TURNING KNOBS OR SLIDING BOLTS IN A SPECIAL SEQUENCE TO UNLOCK THE DOOR.

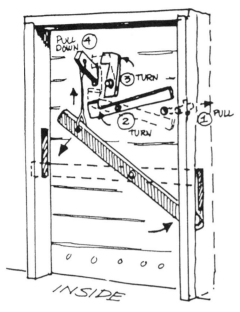

TURN KNOB LOCK

FAKE KNOBS

INSIDE

OUTSIDE

THIS SLIDE BOLT LOCK (BELOW) IS MADE WHILE THE DOOR IS BEING BUILT AND IS COVERED BY THE FRONT DOOR PANEL SO THAT ONLY THE FOUR BOLT HANDLES ARE VISIBLE.

SLIDE BOLT LOCK

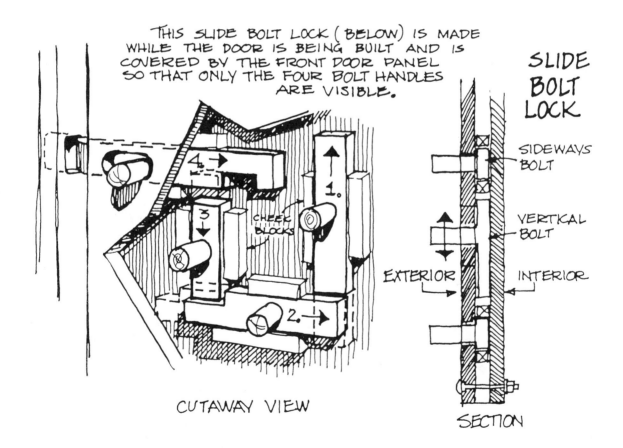

CHEEK BLOCKS

CUTAWAY VIEW

SIDEWAYS BOLT

VERTICAL BOLT

EXTERIOR

INTERIOR

SECTION

Secret Lock Box

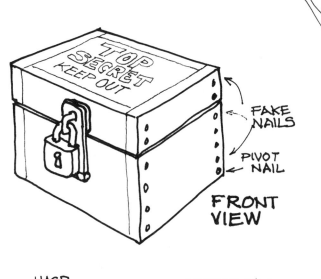

FRONT VIEW

FAKE NAILS

PIVOT NAIL

All kids need a box to keep their secret stuff in. This strong lock box looks impossible to open unless you know the secret. (It is opened in the back by pushing in a special spot).

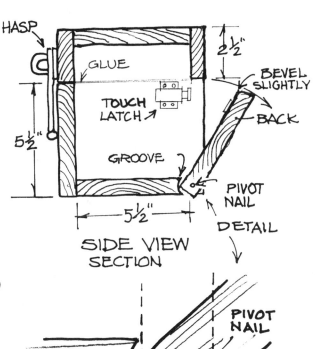

HASP

GLUE

TOUCH LATCH

GROOVE

2½"

BEVEL SLIGHTLY

BACK

5½"

5½"

PIVOT NAIL

SIDE VIEW SECTION

DETAIL

PIVOT NAIL

BOTTOM

BACK

GROOVE

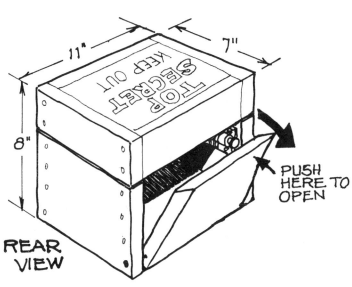

11"

7"

8"

PUSH HERE TO OPEN

REAR VIEW

You can make the secret lock box out of common 1x6 and 1x3 boards. The back piece swings out by means of 2 carefully placed pivot nails. Before putting in the nails, groove the bottom piece so that it won't bind when the back opens (see **side view section**).

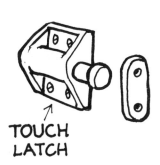

TOUCH LATCH

Birdhouse

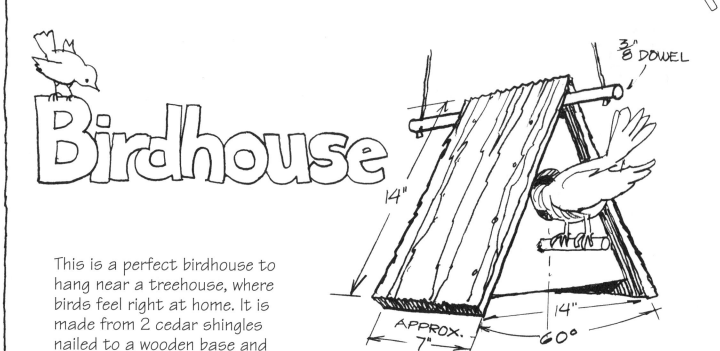

3/8" DOWEL

14"

APPROX. 7"

14"

60°

This is a perfect birdhouse to hang near a treehouse, where birds feel right at home. It is made from 2 cedar shingles nailed to a wooden base and enclosed by front and back walls.

It is a lot easier to make the base if you have a table or miter saw, set at 30 degrees; however, you can also cut it out using a handsaw, if you are careful.

BASE

HINGE

BACK

Hinge the back wall to open out so that it can be cleaned out each year.

Hang the birdhouse from a branch where squirrels can't get at it.

Ring swing game

This simple game can provide hours of fun. Attach it to a branch near your treehouse. Play it with your friends, family or even by yourself. The object is to let the ring swing and catch itself on the hook. One "hook" out of ten tries is EXPERT; one "hook" out of twenty tries is AVERAGE. All you need is a 2-inch ring, a 4-inch screw hook, a 1-inch-long screw eye and a piece of nylon string. Find a branch that is about 8 feet from the ground. Screw the screw eye to the underside of the branch, 4 feet from the trunk of the tree. Screw the 4-inch screw hook to the tree, 5 feet from the ground. Tie one end of the string to the screw hook and the other end to the ring, making sure the center of the ring can pass over the hook when the string is straight. Stand back and hold the ring so that the string is taut and let go. The ring will swing towards the hook on the tree and hopefully catch itself on the hook.
GOOD LUCK!

Tarzan Swing

BRANCH

LOOP

PULL DOWN TO TIGHTEN

This is a great way to get wet fast. All you need is a tree that has a strong branch reaching out over the water and a strong rope. You might even select the spot for your treehouse with this in mind. Tie a loop in the end of a rope and throw it over the branch (using a weight). Place the other end of the rope through the loop and pull it up to the branch. Tie some knots in the bottom end to have something to hold on to.

Snölykta
(SNOW LIGHT)

When snow covers the roof of your treehouse, light up the deck with these snölyktas (snow lights). Or make several of them to light the path that leads to your treehouse. The Swedish custom is to have a snölykta outside one's house as an expression of good cheer. The main idea is to have an enclosure for a candle whose flame sends a warm glow through the snow and out into the night. However, in Sweden, snölyktas often become elaborate sculptures.

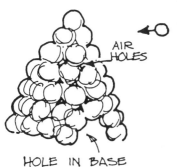

AIR HOLES

HOLE IN BASE FOR CANDLE

The simplest construction is to build a pyramid of snowballs, hollow on the inside, and place a candle in the middle. A more elaborate snölykta can be made by first freezing water into a solid shape and then carving it out with a knife.

Another version dating back to the early 1900s, as told by Ma Karlstrom, is made this way:

Fill a pail with water and allow the inside surface to partially freeze.

Remove the pail and cut a hole in the bottom. Let the water drain out.

Provide an air hole in the bottom for the candle.

Stuff to Do in Your Treehouse

Washtub Fiddle

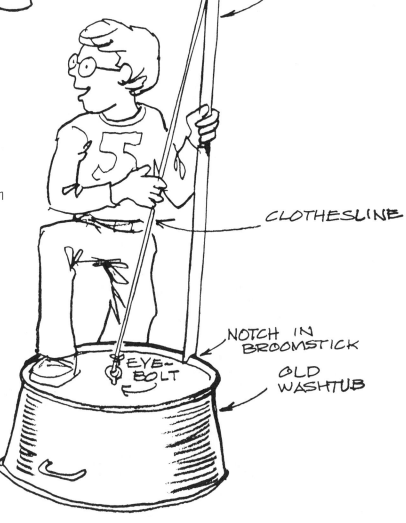

BROOMSTICK

CLOTHESLINE

NOTCH IN BROOMSTICK

EYE-BOLT

OLD WASHTUB

This homemade bass fiddle is played by strumming it with your fingers. It provides a backbeat for voice or guitar. You can change the pitch by bending the broomstick back, which tightens the string.

All you need to make this instrument is a galvanized washtub (see **Resources**), a broomstick, a piece of clothesline and an eyebolt.

Bore a hole in the top end of the broomstick to hold the rope. Notch the bottom end so that it fits on the rim of the washtub. An easy way to do this is to drill a 1/4-inch hole near the bottom of the broomstick and cut through the middle of the hole with a saw.

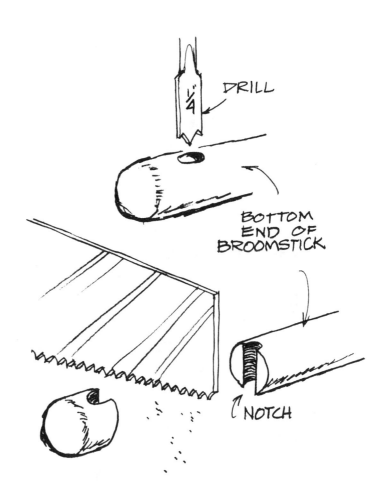

DRILL

BOTTOM END OF BROOMSTICK

NOTCH

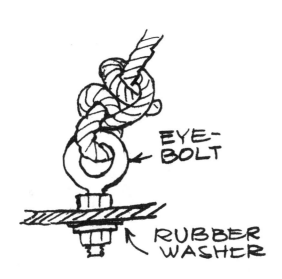

EYE-BOLT

RUBBER WASHER

Bore a 1/4-inch hole in the center of the washtub and attach a 1/4 x 1/4-inch eyebolt. Tie a clothesline rope to the eyebolt and to the top of the broomstick. Strum away!

TOM·TOM

You can make a tom-tom out of almost any large container, but the easiest one to use is a common drywall compound bucket found at most house building sites or at a home improvement center. You will also need an 18 x 18-inch piece of heavy canvas cut into an 18-inch-diameter circle. Make sure it is a heavy unprimed canvas, which you can find in most art supply stores.

FOAM BLOCKS

Prepare the canvas for the drumhead by folding the canvas edges over, approximately 1 1/2 inches. Heat up the tip of a 16d, 3 1/2-inch long, common nail and poke the nail into 2 layers of the canvas at the same time, every 2 1/2 inches.

HOLES MADE WITH A HOT NAIL

(CUT-AWAY VIEW FOR CLARIFICATION)

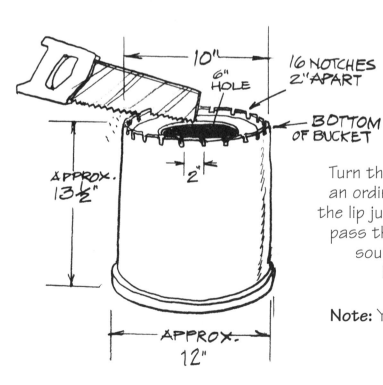

10"

6" HOLE

16 NOTCHES 2" APART

BOTTOM OF BUCKET

APPROX. 13½"

2"

APPROX. 12"

Turn the bucket upside down and, using an ordinary handsaw, cut 16 notches in the lip just wide enough for the string to pass through. To improve the quality of sound, cut a 6-inch-wide hole in the bottom, using an electric jigsaw.

Note: You can also use synthetic skins found in fabric stores or online.

LACING THE DRUMHEAD

Note: Soak the canvas in hot water before lacing it.

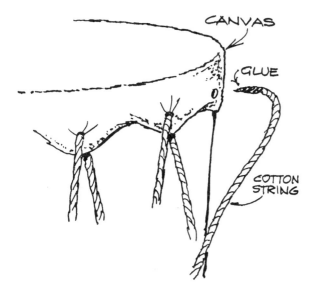

CANVAS

GLUE

COTTON STRING

Cut a piece of heavy cotton string, approximately 50 feet long, to lace the canvas to the bucket. To make the string go into the holes easily, apply white glue to the end, twist it into a point and let it dry. Lace the canvas to the bucket by threading the string through a pair of holes in the top of the canvas, pulling it down through a notch and across the bottom of the bucket, into the notch on the opposite side and back up into another pair of holes in the canvas. Continue lacing the canvas to the bucket, pulling the string as tight as possible while you work.

Tighten the drumhead by inserting rigid foam blocks between the strings and the side of the bucket (see illustration on previous page).

Make the drumstick out of two 3/8-inch-diameter dowels, approximately 10 inches long. The ball on the end can be anything from a rubber handball or sponge ball to a golf ball. Clamp the ball in a vise while drilling a 3/8-inch hole in the ball. If you are using a golf ball, be prepared that some juice may squirt out from inside it while you are drilling.

DRUMSTICK

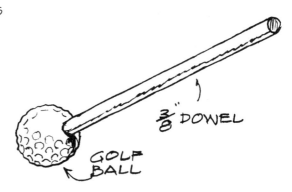

$\frac{3}{8}$" DOWEL

GOLF BALL

CROW CALL

A unique way to signal friends when you are up in your treehouse is to use a piece of grass to make a sound similar to a crow's call. Find a flat piece of grass about 1/4 inch wide and 3 inches long. Place the piece of grass between both thumbs and the heel of your hand and stretch it lengthwise. Place your mouth against the opening between your 2 hands and blow hard!

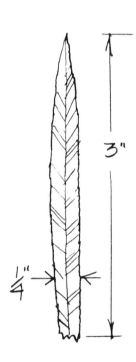

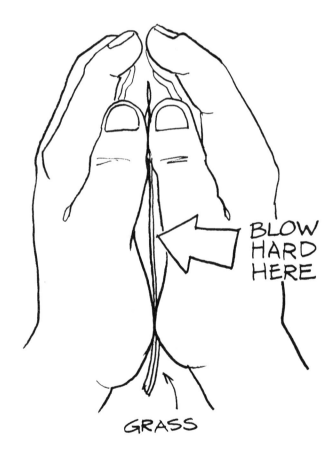

BLOW HARD HERE

GRASS

The blade of grass acts like the reed of a musical wind instrument.

NOISEMAKER

If you want to make a very disagreeable noise, try making this noisemaker.

Find an empty tin can (the bigger the better) and punch a hole in the bottom using a nail and a hammer.

Poke a string through the hole and tie a stop knot in the end of the string.

Wet an old piece of towel or washcloth and, while holding the cloth over your hand, grab the string very tightly and pull down hard. This is a good way to signal to friends that you are in your treehouse (or to scare away enemies). It will make a sound unlike anything you've heard before.

Tip: You might want to put cotton in your ears first!

WOOD MUSIC

This easy-to-make wooden musical instrument can be a perfect addition to your treehouse, suspended from an overhanging branch. The sound it makes is soft and melodic, similar to a marimba, and will not offend birds or neighbors.

Rip cut each bar from a 1-inch-thick, 5/4-inch hardwood board, like mahogany. Drill a 1/8-inch hole through the top ends of the wooden pieces, 3/4 inch down from the top. Thread a thin stainless wire through the holes and attach the 2 ends to the tree, as shown.

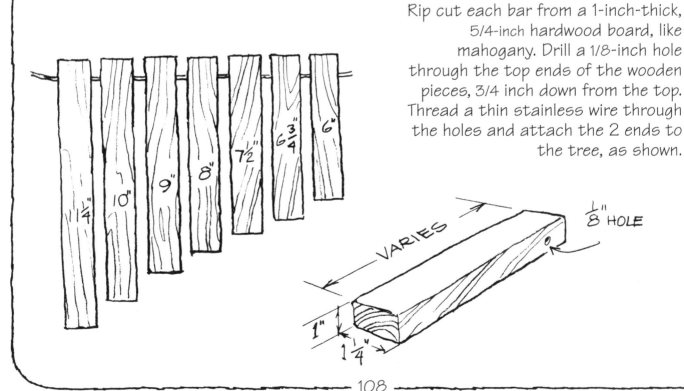

11¼"   10"   9"   8"   7½"   6¾"   6"

VARIES

1"

1¼"

⅛" HOLE

Weekend Projects

Lemonade Stand

75¢

Lemonade

This lemonade stand is simply a box made from scrap lumber, attached to an old bicycle wheel. The dimensions we used are based on a 12-inch-diameter wheel. If your wheel is a different size, you can adjust the height of the front bracket support (see sketch) to make the box level.

CUT OUT NOTCH FOR WHEEL IF NECESSARY

FRONT BRACKET SUPPORT

2X2 AXLE SUPPORT

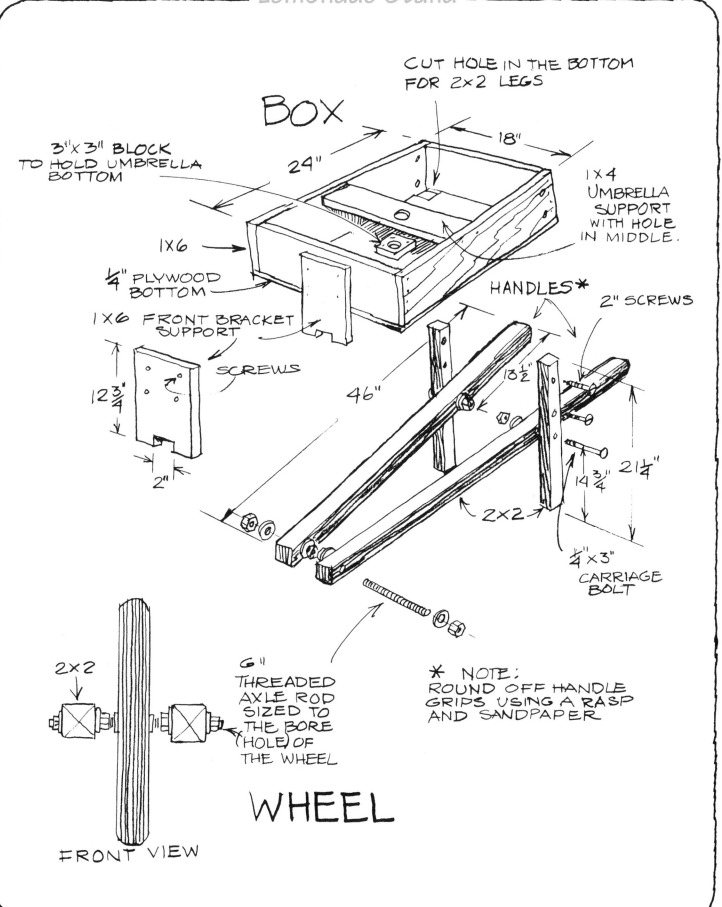

CUT HOLE IN THE BOTTOM FOR 2×2 LEGS

BOX

3"×3" BLOCK TO HOLD UMBRELLA BOTTOM

24"

18"

1×4 UMBRELLA SUPPORT WITH HOLE IN MIDDLE.

1×6

1/4" PLYWOOD BOTTOM

1×6 FRONT BRACKET SUPPORT

SCREWS

12 3/4"

2"

HANDLES *

2" SCREWS

46"

13 1/2"

21 1/4"

14 3/4"

2×2

1/4"×3" CARRIAGE BOLT

2×2

6" THREADED AXLE ROD SIZED TO THE BORE (HOLE) OF THE WHEEL

* NOTE: ROUND OFF HANDLE GRIPS USING A RASP AND SANDPAPER

WHEEL

FRONT VIEW

111

GETTING STARTED

YOU WILL NEED:

☐ A LARGE PITCHER TO POUR THE LEMONADE

☐ A LONG WOODEN SPOON TO MIX IT

☐ SEVERAL PACKAGES OF INSTANT LEMONADE

☐ ICE CUBES IN A BUCKET

☐ SMALL PAPER CUPS (AT LEAST 2 DOZEN)

☐ A NOTEBOOK AND PENCIL

☐ A CASH BOX

(AN OLD CIGAR BOX WITH SLOTS CUT IN THE TOP AND DIVIDERS INSIDE)

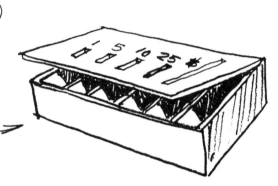

OPTIONAL: A RAIN UMBRELLA OR BEACH UMBRELLA AND A SIGN TO WAVE AT MOTORISTS.

STRAIGHT UMBRELLA

AUTHORS' NOTE:
ALTHOUGH INSTANT LEMONADE IS FINE, THERE IS NOTHING BETTER THAN REAL LEMONADE MADE WITH REAL LEMONS, SUGAR AND WATER.
(CHARGE EXTRA IF YOU USE REAL LEMONS).

Mind Your Own Business

If you are starting your own business selling lemonade, here are some things you should know before beginning.

Materials
If you're not making lemonade from real lemons, check your kitchen to see if you have any instant lemonade. If the cupboard is bare, use your allowance to buy some lemonade and small paper cups.

Sales and Profit
Keep track of your sales on a pad of paper and at the end of the day, subtract your costs (cups, lemonade, maybe cookies). You will be left with your profit.

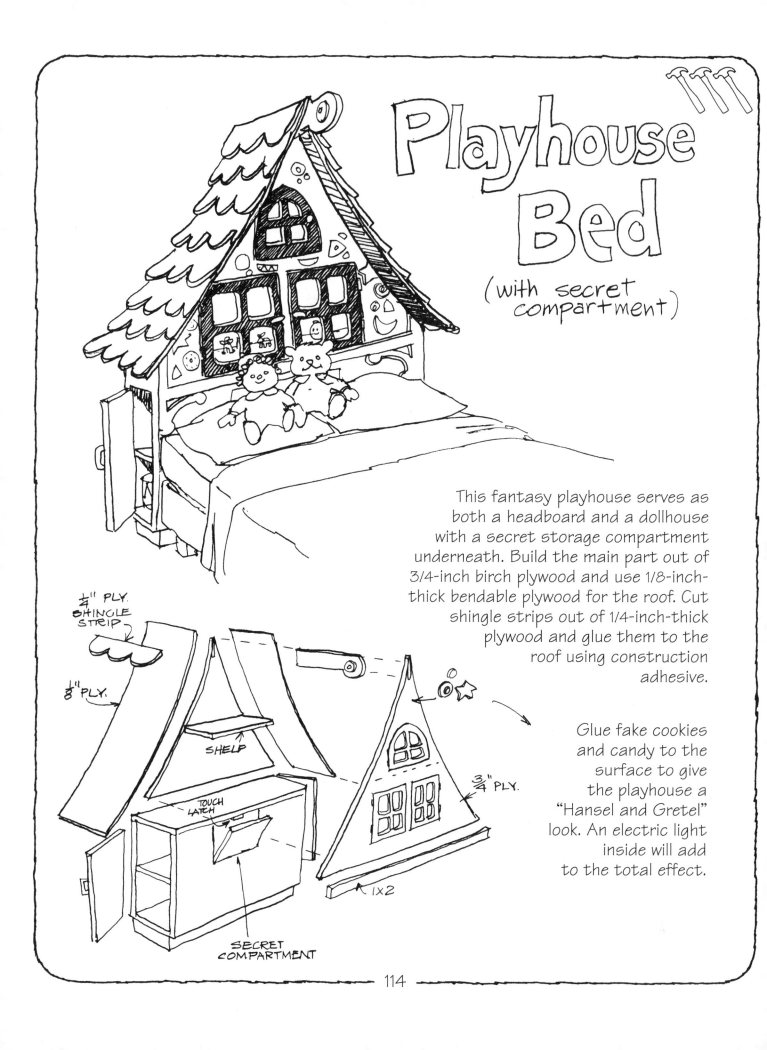

Playhouse Bed

(with secret compartment)

¼" PLY. SHINGLE STRIP

⅛" PLY.

SHELF

¾" PLY.

TOUCH LATCH

1x2

SECRET COMPARTMENT

This fantasy playhouse serves as both a headboard and a dollhouse with a secret storage compartment underneath. Build the main part out of 3/4-inch birch plywood and use 1/8-inch-thick bendable plywood for the roof. Cut shingle strips out of 1/4-inch-thick plywood and glue them to the roof using construction adhesive.

Glue fake cookies and candy to the surface to give the playhouse a "Hansel and Gretel" look. An electric light inside will add to the total effect.

Fake Bar Bells

These barbells actually only weigh a few pounds. What appear to be heavy weights are actually Styrofoam disks, available at novelty and craft stores.
The bar can be made from an old broomstick or PVC plastic pipe. Glue the Styrofoam disks together with a special glue for Styrofoam sold at home-building supply centers. Paint them flat black to look like cast iron.

This is a great idea for birthday parties! Take photos for party favors.

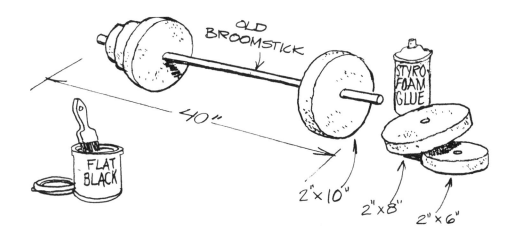

OLD BROOMSTICK

40"

STYRO FOAM GLUE

FLAT BLACK

2" x 10"

2" x 8"

2" x 6"

Exploding Cannon

This harmless cannon delivers a blast of white smoke and shoots a foam ball about 10 feet into the air. It is made of pieces of inexpensive drainpipe, two 10-foot pieces of 2x3 lumber and some scrap plywood. A CO_2 fire extinguisher, hidden beneath the barrel, propels the ball out of the cannon barrel and delivers a large WHOOSH of harmless (cold) vapor. You can often find secondhand CO_2 fire extinguishers by calling your local fire department and asking them where they get theirs recharged. CO_2 fire extinguishers are being phased out, so there should be a lot of used ones for sale at a cheap price. Only the 17-inch-long CO_2 fire extinguishers are the right size for these plans. Recharging them costs approximately $15.

Barrel

Making the barrel of the cannon is very simple. Ask your plumbing supply store to cut you 2 pieces of 4-inch PVC pipe, one 10 1/2 inches long and the other 12 inches long. Buy 2 PVC couplings and a PVC cap to fit over the pipe. Also, buy 10 inches of 1 1/2-inch-diameter PVC pipe for the pivot posts and a small can of PVC cement. Using a handsaw, cut 2 1/2-inches off one of the couplings to fit over the front piece of pipe. Glue the pieces together, as shown in the illustration. Drill 1 1/2-inch-diameter holes in the sides of the middle coupling for the pivot posts and glue them in place.

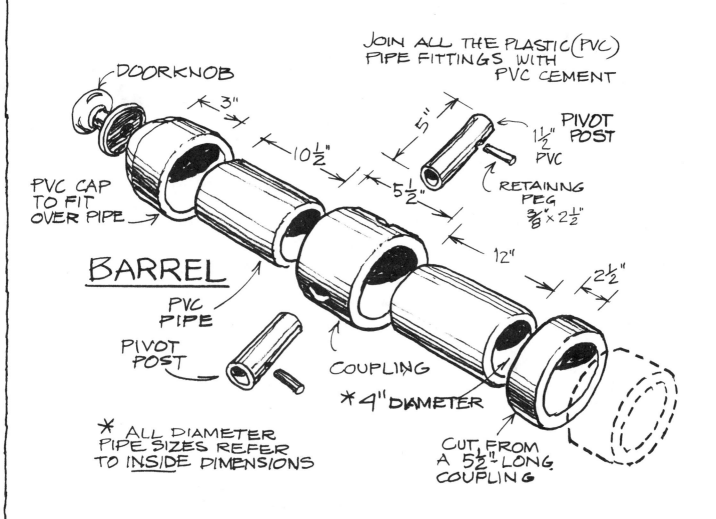

DOORKNOB

JOIN ALL THE PLASTIC (PVC)
PIPE FITTINGS WITH
PVC CEMENT

3"

5"

PIVOT
POST
1½"
PVC

10½"

5½"

RETAINNG
PEG
⅜" × 2½"

PVC CAP
TO FIT
OVER PIPE

12"

2½"

BARREL

PVC
PIPE

PIVOT
POST

COUPLING

* 4" DIAMETER

CUT FROM
A 5½" LONG
COUPLING

* ALL DIAMETER
PIPE SIZES REFER
TO INSIDE DIMENSIONS

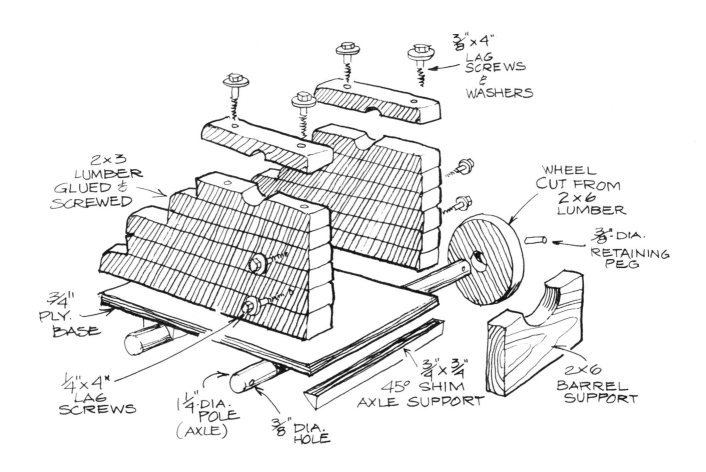

Within the diagram, the following labels appear:

- 3/8" x 4" LAG SCREWS & WASHERS
- 2x3 LUMBER GLUED & SCREWED
- WHEEL CUT FROM 2x6 LUMBER
- 3/8" DIA. RETAINING PEG
- 3/4" PLY. BASE
- 1/4" x 4" LAG SCREWS
- 1 1/4"-DIA. POLE (AXLE)
- 3/8" DIA. HOLE
- 3/4" x 3/4" 45° SHIM AXLE SUPPORT
- 2x6 BARREL SUPPORT

Base

Build the base using 2x3s for the sides and 3/4-inch plywood for the floor. Cut the wheels and the barrel support piece from 2x6 lumber. Cut and screw the 2x3 pieces together and to the plywood base from underneath. Attach the sides to the 2x6 barrel support piece using four 4-inch-long, 1/4-inch-diameter lag screws. Cut the 1 1/4-inch-diameter poles for the wheels, allowing them to extend 3/4 inch past the wheels. Allow 1/8 inch clearance for the wheels to turn without rubbing against the sides. Bore the holes in the wheels slightly larger so that the wheels turn freely.

Screw the axle poles to the bottom of the plywood base. To strengthen the joint where the axle meets the bottom of the base, cut four 12-inch-long wood shim strips at 45-degree angles and glue them to both sides of each axle. Bore 3/8-inch-diameter holes in the ends of the axle poles and insert 3/8-inch-diameter retaining pegs to hold the wheels.

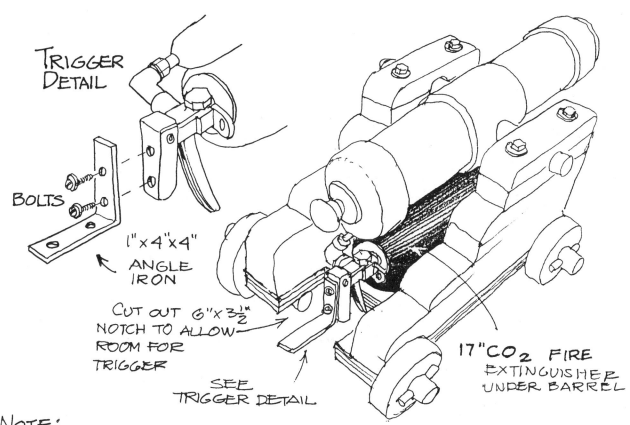

TRIGGER DETAIL

BOLTS

1"x4"x4" ANGLE IRON

CUT OUT 6"x3½" NOTCH TO ALLOW ROOM FOR TRIGGER

SEE TRIGGER DETAIL

17" CO_2 FIRE EXTINGUISHER UNDER BARREL

NOTE:

THE PURPOSE OF THE ANGLE IRON IS TO GIVE MORE LEVERAGE TO THE TRIGGER.

CUT HOLE IN BOTTOM OF THE BARREL TO ALLOW FOR INSERTION OF FIRE EXTINGUISHER HORN.

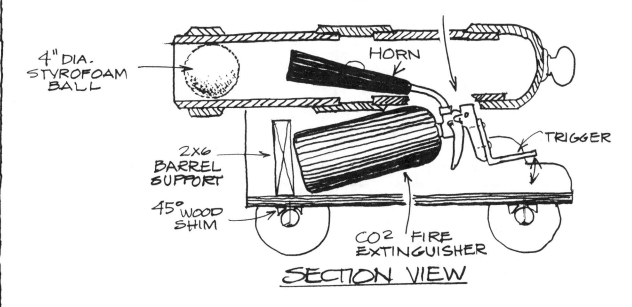

4" DIA. STYROFOAM BALL

HORN

TRIGGER

2x6 BARREL SUPPORT

45° WOOD SHIM

CO_2 FIRE EXTINGUISHER

SECTION VIEW

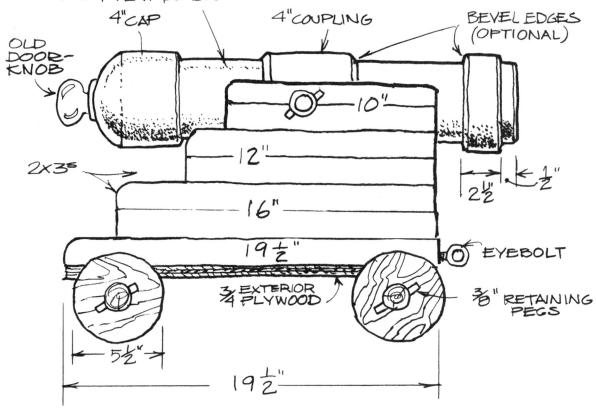

SAND ALL PVC SURFACES TO REMOVE GLOSS AND PAINT FLAT BLACK

4" CAP

4" COUPLING

BEVEL EDGES (OPTIONAL)

OLD DOOR-KNOB

10"

2x3ˢ

12"

16"

19½"

2½" ½"

19½"

5½"

¾ EXTERIOR PLYWOOD

EYEBOLT

⅜" RETAINING PEGS

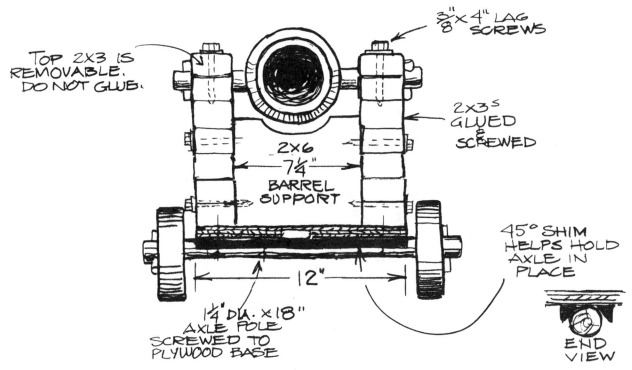

TOP 2x3 IS REMOVABLE. DO NOT GLUE.

⅜" x 4" LAG SCREWS

2x3ˢ GLUED & SCREWED

2x6 7¼" BARREL SUPPORT

45° SHIM HELPS HOLD AXLE IN PLACE

12"

1¼" DIA. x 18" AXLE POLE SCREWED TO PLYWOOD BASE

END VIEW

ALKA ROCKET

This paper rocket is completely harmless and makes a good science experiment. It is propelled by a 1/4 tablet of Alka Seltzer combined with a small amount of water in a plastic film canister. This mixture produces CO_2, which expands, forcing the lid to suddenly pop off and sending the rocket as much as 10 feet in the air.

All you need are 4 sheets of 8 1/2 x 11-inch letter paper, a 35mm film canister, 1 Alka Seltzer tablet, some Scotch tape and a little white glue. It takes about 15 minutes to put this together.

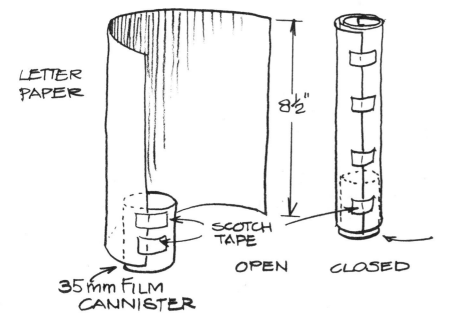

LETTER PAPER

8½"

SCOTCH TAPE

OPEN

CLOSED

35mm FILM CANNISTER

Start by attaching one end of an 8 1/2 x 11-inch piece of paper around a film canister (white Fuji 35mm canisters are the best). Continue wrapping the paper around the canister and tape it closed. Allow a tiny bit of the canister to stick out at the bottom.

NOSE CONE

Make the nose cone by drawing a 2 1/2-inch-radius circle onto a second piece of paper. Cut out the circle and make a straight cut to its center. Bend the paper to form a cone and secure it with tape or white glue. Glue the cone to the top of the rocket.

2½"

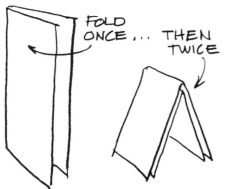

NOSE CONE

FINS

Fold a third piece of paper in half and then in half again. Draw a line down its center and cut it in half.

FOLD ONCE... THEN TWICE

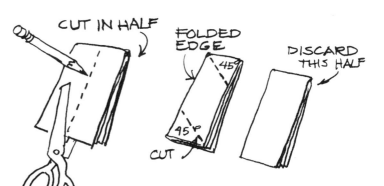

CUT IN HALF

FOLDED EDGE

45°

DISCARD THIS HALF

45°

CUT

Draw 45-degree parallel angles at 2 opposite corners of each folded paper and cut them off. You should end up with 2 fins. Repeat the above steps to make additional fins, for a total of 4 fins.

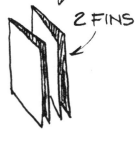

2 FINS

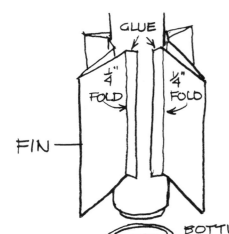

GLUE

¼" FOLD   ¼" FOLD

FIN

BOTTLE CAP

NOTE: THE BOTTOM OF THE FINS SHOULD TOUCH THE GROUND WHEN THE ROCKET IS STANDING UP.

Launching

Choose a day when there is little or no wind. Take the rocket outside along with a measuring cup filled with water and a tablet of Alka Seltzer. Break the tablet into 4 equal pieces. Turn the rocket upside down and fill the canister 1/3 full with water. Quickly drop a 1/4 tablet into the water and snap on the cap. Stand the rocket right side up on a level surface. Stand back and count down approximately 15 seconds until liftoff. You will hear a loud POP, and the rocket will shoot up into the air.

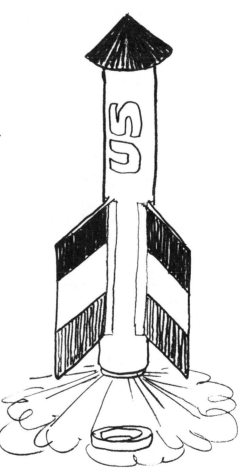

To make the rocket more impressive, paint the nose cone red and the fins red, white and blue.

INSPIRED BY GORDON BRADFORD

Totem Pole

2 X 12 PINE

12" to 14" DIAMETER LOG

If you like to carve or paint, then this is the project for you. Totem poles were a Native American tradition in the Pacific Northwest. Generally, they told a story about a family's background. You can carve your totem pole to reflect your personal interests—like your family dog, your astrological sign, or your favorite animals, birds or flowers.

To carve a totem pole, you will need several sharp chisels of different sizes, a mallet and lots of patience. You can add to the totem pole by mortising and doweling pieces to the main post, as shown in the illustration. Let this project show off your personal skills and creativity.

Cool Bike

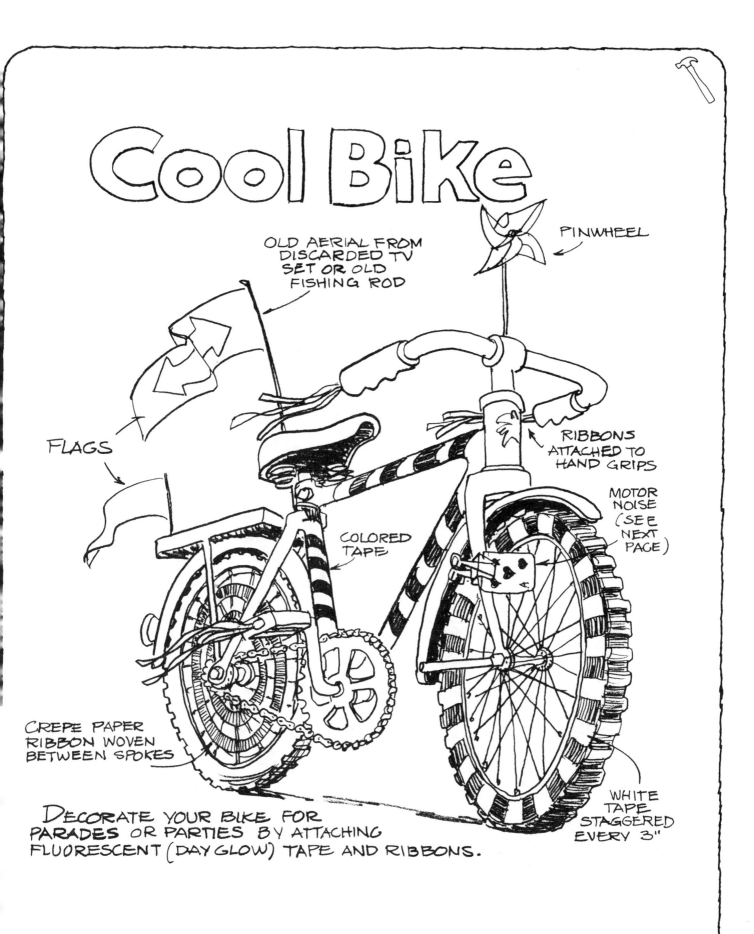

PINWHEEL

OLD AERIAL FROM DISCARDED TV SET OR OLD FISHING ROD

FLAGS

RIBBONS ATTACHED TO HAND GRIPS

MOTOR NOISE (SEE NEXT PAGE)

COLORED TAPE

CREPE PAPER RIBBON WOVEN BETWEEN SPOKES

WHITE TAPE STAGGERED EVERY 3"

DECORATE YOUR BIKE FOR PARADES OR PARTIES BY ATTACHING FLUORESCENT (DAY GLOW) TAPE AND RIBBONS.

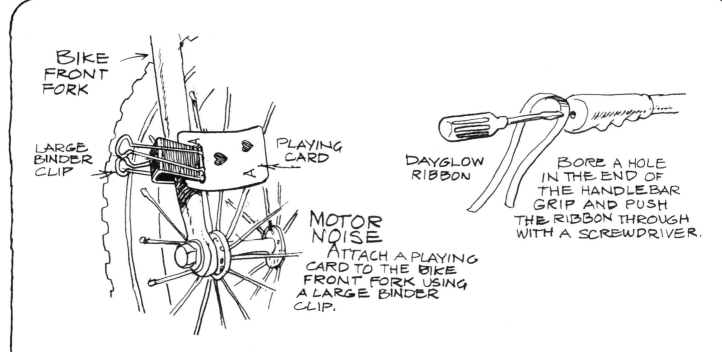

BIKE FRONT FORK

LARGE BINDER CLIP

PLAYING CARD

DAYGLOW RIBBON

BORE A HOLE IN THE END OF THE HANDLEBAR GRIP AND PUSH THE RIBBON THROUGH WITH A SCREWDRIVER.

MOTOR NOISE

ATTACH A PLAYING CARD TO THE BIKE FRONT FORK USING A LARGE BINDER CLIP.

TO MAKE A PINWHEEL

CUT A PIECE OF PAPER INTO A SQUARE

FOLD THE PAPER IN HALF DIAGONALLY...

..THEN FOLD IT AGAIN ...

... AND THEN UNFOLD IT.

CUT ALONG THE FOLDS THREE-QUARTERS TO THE CENTER.

PUSHPIN

PUNCH HOLES TO THE RIGHT SIDE OF THE CUTS AT THE CORNERS, AS SHOWN ABOVE.

PUSH THE PIN THROUGH THE CORNER HOLES AND THROUGH THE CENTER AND INTO THE RUBBER END OF A NEW PENCIL.

PENCIL

Sweet Tooth Tiger

Thousands of years
ago, there existed a
creature feared by man
and beast alike. His roar
shook the forest and his
thrashing and stomping could
be heard from miles around. So
feared was this monster that sacrifices had to be made
to keep him under control. Oddly enough, the only thing that would
stop him from destroying everything in sight was candy, hence the name
"Sweet Tooth Tiger." Only the bravest child could give him the treats as
this required reaching through his enormous teeth and leaving the candy
in his mouth! Anthropologists thought this creature was extinct, but
recent sightings have been reported, especially around Halloween. So keep
a watchful eye out for the Sweet Tooth Tiger and make sure to feed him
candy if he should suddenly appear.

The Sweet Tooth Tiger can be made using 1-inch chicken wire covered with papier-mâché. The main head bone and lower jawbone are hinged together with a 3/8-inch wooden dowel. The teeth are made out of soft foam rubber to prevent injuries. Small penlights or red bicycle reflectors can be inserted in the eyes to make the tiger scarier at night.

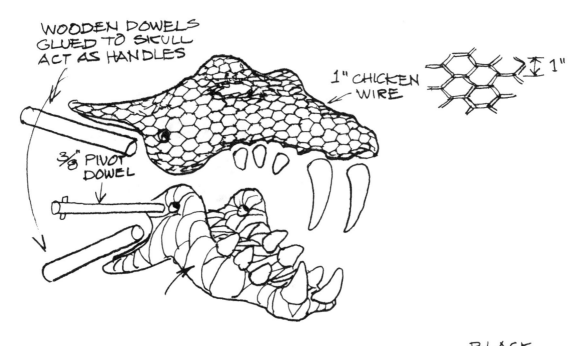

WOODEN DOWELS GLUED TO SKULL ACT AS HANDLES

1" CHICKEN WIRE

3/8" PIVOT DOWEL

Papier-mâché is used to make a hard skin over a chicken wire base. It is made by ripping (not cutting) strips of newspaper dipped in white glue or wallpaper paste. Overlap and criss-cross the strips until they are three or four layers thick. Add rolled-up balls of paper towels to create bumps where needed. For a harder-surfaced coating, you can use plaster, Polyester resin or auto body dent filler.

BLACK CLOAK

The Ugliest, Best, Cheapest Desk Lamp in the World

One reason this lamp is so great is that it can be bent to shine in any direction. The curvy thing that looks like a snake is actually a brass gas flex hose that plumbers use to connect stoves to gas lines. Plumbers throw them away every time they change a stove. Ask your plumber for an old one or buy one from a plumbing supply store. The lamp socket and lamp cord are very inexpensive and easily available. Make the shade using an old soup or tomato can. You can make the lamp even uglier by adding ping-pong balls for eyes and painting it weird colors.

Important tip: Drill several holes in the back of the can to relieve the heat from the inside.

TIN CAN

SWITCH

TOMATO SAUCE

GAS FLEX PIPE

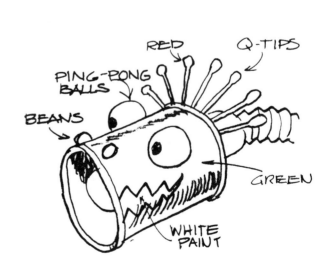

RED

Q-TIPS

PING-PONG BALLS

BEANS

GREEN

WHITE PAINT

BULB

BRASS
SOCKET
SHELL

PAPER
INSULATOR

LAMP
SOCKET

SILVER
SCREW

NEUTRAL
WIRE

RIBS

SOCKET
CAP

SWITCH

BRASS
SCREW

HOT
WIRE

UNDERWRITER'S
KNOT

EPOXY OR
POLYURETHANE
GLUE

FLEX GAS
PIPE

ASSEMBLY

- Feed a 7-foot-long lamp cord through a 48-inch-long gas flex pipe.
- Strip 5/8 inch of insulation off the ends of the wire and twist them tight.
- Insert the wire through the socket cap and tie a knot.
- Separate the wires and find the wire that is neutral.

Hint: The neutral wire is the one that has tiny ribs running lengthwise (barely visible).

- Connect this wire to the silver screw and the other wire to the brass screw.
- Slip on the paper insulator sleeve and the brass socket shell.
- Screw in the bulb.

SHADE

Find an old tomato can (29 oz.) and drill a 1/2-inch-diameter hole in the bottom. Use tin snips to cut and bend in tabs around the hole so that the socket will fit into it snugly. Attach the can to the lamp socket with epoxy.

TIP.   CUT AND BEND IN TABS, THEN ATTACH THE CAN TO THE LAMP SOCKET WITH EPOXY OR POLYURE-THANE GLUE.

29 OZ.
TOMATO CAN

TIN SNIPS

BAT SIGNAL

This showstopper is a great Halloween
project for kids and adults alike.
Use this bat signal as a cool beacon
to lead your guests to your Halloween
party, and your party will be remembered
for years to come. If your parents still
have an old slide projector stored in the attic, ask them if you can borrow it for
the night and set up this bat signal. Make your own slide by drawing in ink a bat
signal or any other scary image (a vampire, skeleton or witch) on clear acetate.
Mount it on a cardboard slide that fits into the projector. Project the slide out of
your window onto any flat object, like the house across the street, or onto a bed
sheet hung between 2 trees in the front yard.

Cootie Catcher

This is a neat trick to play on your friends. Make this cootie catcher from a square piece of paper and draw tiny "cooties" (make-believe lice) on 4 of the inside triangles. Hold the cootie catcher in your hand and show your friend the blank triangles inside the cootie catcher, and then place it on his head to "catch the cooties" in his hair. Open it again, this time exposing the triangles with the cooties on them.

Making the Cootie Catcher

Cut an ordinary piece of letter-size paper so it forms a perfect square. Draw diagonal lines from corner to corner to find the center.

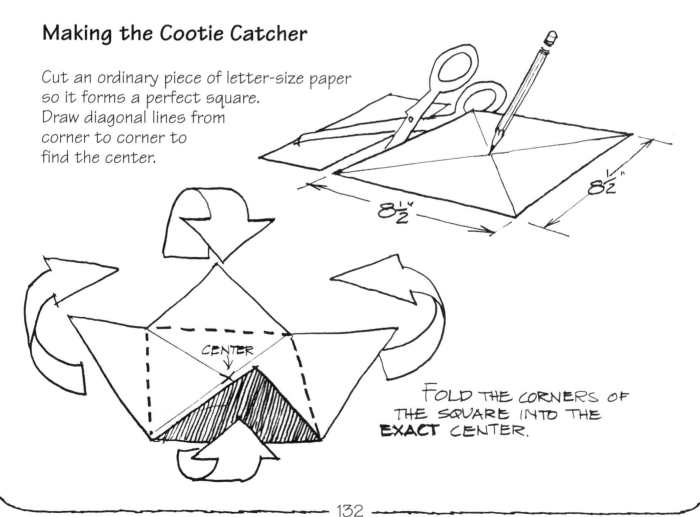

CENTER

FOLD THE CORNERS OF THE SQUARE INTO THE **EXACT** CENTER.

$8\frac{1}{2}$"

$8\frac{1}{2}$"

TURN IT OVER AND FOLD
THE CORNERS INTO THE
CENTER AGAIN.

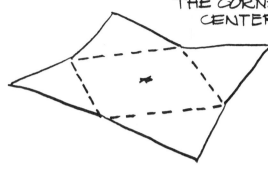

FOLD THE
SQUARE IN HALF
ONE WAY...
... AND THEN IN HALF
THE OTHER WAY.

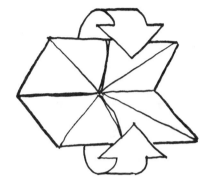

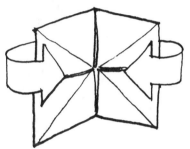

TURN IT OVER AND
PUSH THE CENTER UNDERNEATH
TO SPREAD THE FOUR POINTS
OPEN.

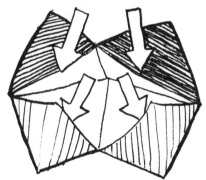

PLACE YOUR THUMB AND
THREE FINGERS IN THE FOUR
TRIANGULAR POCKETS AND
SQUEEZE TO FORM THE
COOTIE CATCHER.

Wheel of Fortune

This game is easily made from a discarded bicycle wheel and some old lumber. Attach the wheel to a 2x6 board, using a lag screw and washers. Make the numbers by first cutting out and sticking pieces of 1 1/2-inch-wide red plastic tape to the tire and then applying white 3/4-inch-wide plastic numbers to the tape. The tape and numbers are sold at most hardware stores.

Have an adult cut a rectangular piece from the corner of a plastic milk carton and screw it to the 2x6 board to create a rachet noise when you spin the wheel and to stop the wheel from turning.

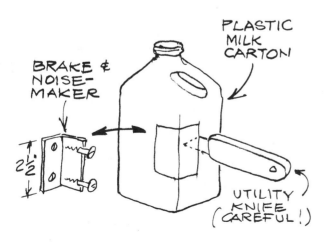

BRAKE & NOISE-MAKER

2½

PLASTIC MILK CARTON

UTILITY KNIFE (CAREFUL!)

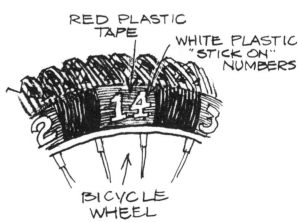

RED PLASTIC TAPE

WHITE PLASTIC "STICK ON" NUMBERS

BICYCLE WHEEL

Resources

Hardware, Lumber and Tools

Antique Hardware
Van Dyke's Restorers
800-558-1234
www.vandykes.com

Hand Tools
Harbor Freight Tools
800-423-2567
www.harborfreight.com
Cable cutters, socket wrenches, jacks, come-alongs and inner tubes

Lumber and Hardware
Lowe's Company, Inc.
800-445-8641
www.lowes.com

Power Tools
Hitachi Koki USA, Ltd.
800-206-7337
www.hitachi-koki.com
Cordless drills and miter saws

Pressure-Treated Wood Stain/Sealer
Osmose Wood Preserving, Inc.
716-882-5905
www.osmose.com

Other Good Resources

American Flags Express
262-783-4800
www.flagsexpress.com
A source for all kinds of flags

MAKE magazine
707-827-7000
www.makezine.com
A how-to magazine with great ideas and clear instructions for making far-out high-tech gadgets

R&W Rope Warehouse
866-577-5505
www.rwrope.com
Hempex (synthetic hemp-like tan rope)

Samson Rope Technologies
800-227-7673
360-384-4669
Nylon rope and technical advice

Titebond III Glue
800-347-4583
www.titebond.com

Barn Sash Windows
Recycled Products
800-765-1489
www.recycledproductsco.com
Recycled and custom sizes, made from recycled plastic milk bottles

Specific Items for Projects in the Book

Agri-Direct
800-345 0169
www.agri-supply.com
Reasonably priced wheels
Downhill Racer: *item #10572*

AM Leonard
800-543-8955
www.amleo.com
Trolley Ride: *lag screw hooks*

Defender Marine & Boat Supplies
800-628-8225
www.defender.com
Pogo Boat: nylon rope, shackles, wire cables and oarlocks
Trolley Ride: braided rope
Merry-Go-Round: dock edging

McMaster-Carr Supply Company
609-259-8900
www.mcmaster.com
Trolley Ride: blocks and pulleys—item #3071 T3
Washtub Fiddle: galvanized tubs—item #4126T4
Treasure Chest: steel ring bolts—item #3047T7 1

Northern Tool & Equipment
800-533-5545
www.northerntool.com
Merry-Go-Round: 2-inch rigid casters

Strike First Corp of America
540-636-4444
www.strikefirstusa.com
Exploding Cannon: CO_2 5-pound fire extinguisher

The Craft Place
616-364-5537
www.thecraftplace.com
Model Sailboat: Styrofoam slabs and glue

Woodcraft
800-535-4486
www.woodcraft.com
Downhill Racer: bullet type ball bearing rollers

Woodworker's Supply, Inc.
800-321-9841
woodworker.com
Hardware
Secret Box: touch latch

Cool Web Sites to Check Out

www.evolutionnyc.com
Prehistoric skulls and weird old skeletons

www.redbullsoapboxusa.com
Crazy soapbox derby cars

www.howtoons.com
Projects you can make—cartoon style

www.industructables.com
More cool stuff you can make

Google: Theo Jensen's Kinetic Sculpture
Fantastic sculptures that actually move

www.UQBARDINK.com
Plans for 6', 7', 8' and 10' superlight prams, using the stitch-and-glue method of construction